LONELINESS IS
NOT FOREVER

LONELINESS IS NOT FOREVER

By
JAMES L. JOHNSON

AUTHOR OF:
Code Name Sebastian
The Nine Lives of Alphonse
A Handful of Dominoes
A Piece of the Moon Is Missing
The Death of Kings
Before Honor
The Nine to Five Complex
What Every Woman Should Know About a Man

MOODY PRESS

CHICAGO

Library of Congress Cataloging in Publication Data

Johnson, James Leonard, 1927-
   Loneliness is not forever.

   Includes bibliographical references.

   1. Loneliness. I. Title.

BV4911.J63   248'.86   79-368

ISBN 0-8024-4949-2

Second Printing, 1979

*To all those who made me
feel I belonged*

Acknowledgments

Quoted material on page 99 is reprinted with the permission of Farrar, Straus & Giroux, Inc., from PROMISES TO KEEP by Agnes W. Dooley. Copyright © 1962 by Agnes W. Dooley and Malcolm W. Dooley. Copyright © 1961 by the Estate of Thomas A. Dooley.

Reprinted on pages 43, 110-11, 168-70 are quotations from CONQUERING LONELINESS by Jean Rosenbaum, M.D., and Veryl Rosenbaum. Copyright © 1973 by Jean Rosenbaum, M.D., and Veryl Rosenbaum. By permission of Hawthorn Books, Inc.

Reprinted on pages 21, 123-24, 131-32 are quotations from ESCAPE FROM LONELINESS by Paul Tournier. Copyright © MCMLXII, W. L. Jenkins. Used by permission of The Westminster Press.

Reprinted on pages 15-17, 34-35, 36, 38, 80, 103-4, 114, 116, 120, 159-60, 180 are specified excerpts (passim) from TO CONQUER LONELINESS by Harold Blake Walker. Copyright © 1966 by Harold B. Walker. By permission of Harper & Row, Publishers, Inc.

Reprinted on pages 126-27 are quotations from LONELY IN AMERICA by Suzanne Gordon. Copyright © 1976 by Suzanne Gordon. Reprinted by permission of Simon & Schuster, a Division of Gulf & Western Corporation.

On page 36 the lines from T. S. Eliot, THE COCKTAIL PARTY, are reprinted by permission of Harcourt Brace Jovanovich, Inc., publisher.

The poem from *Psalms of My Life* by Joseph Bayly, appearing on pages 33-34, is reprinted by permission of Tyndale House Publishers.

Reprinted on pages 103-5 are specified excerpts from SHADOW OF THE ALMIGHTY by Elisabeth Elliot. Copyright © 1958 by Elisabeth Elliot. By permission of Harper & Row, Publishers, Inc.

On page 144, material quoted from *Loneliness and Love* by Clark E. Moustakas (Prentice-Hall, 1972) is reprinted by permission of the publisher.

On pages 182-83, 186, the quotation from *Loneliness* by Clark E. Moustakas (Prentice-Hall, 1961) is reprinted by permission of the publisher.

On pages 15, 31-32, 38, quotations from "Loneliness" by William Sadler, Jr., appearing in *Science Digest*, July 1975, are reprinted by permission of the author.

Contents

ONE

The Mystery of Loneliness

The big frustration is in trying to understand it. It's like chasing a soap bubble in the breeze. Catching one proves nothing; it is only a smear of chemicals that remains in an amorphous state. Like that soap bubble, loneliness can defy definition. It is not enough to say of the soap bubble that it is made up of soap and water; the mystery is in how it comes to be, and how it exists in its floating cocoon.

What is this "it" that hangs on people like a persistent purple cloud, a feeling that cannot be traced to any specific thing, chemically or physically? Not many admit to experiencing it, because it is too difficult to pin down, to define—something that does not fit the parameters of life. Yet every person gets it in one form or another.

There is, again, for those who suffer from it, no vaccination against it, no surgical cure. "Pills and injections" are temporary measures and cause more harm than good in many cases. It continues, meanwhile, to boggle the mind. It lies heavy on the bright, cheerful, and successful as well as on the poor, the failures, the shy, and the withdrawn. It can dog a man or a woman for a lifetime, if allowed. For others it comes at certain times, certain days, triggered by sights or sounds or catastrophic events.

Loneliness.

It is called by many names by those who refuse to admit to experiencing it. But it remains the same, the ever-pervading

9

shadow of melancholia, the heavy hand that smothers the vi-
tality of living, at least for those who let it.

It comes in the form of a "pang of nostalgia," or serious illness born out of mourning, or continual failure, or loss of fulfillment, or just plain loss of companionship that has meaning.
What Americans in general do not realize is that it can kill.

For instance, there is that peaceful southern town where
the people will remember forever the day a sniper's bullet
cut down innocent people in the streets, leaving many dead
and many others wounded. Why a young man of twenty-
four should climb into a city-square tower and kill people
indiscriminately is still a mystery. He did not live to explain
it, and perhaps he could not, even if he had lived. But later,
authorities, after piecing that young man's life together,
found that he was a "loner," or more particularly a person who
had "lost touch with humanity or human values." Loneliness
had driven him to a rage that ended in tragedy for himself and
others.

And again there is the case of a woman forty-three years of
age, a successful stockbroker in Chicago, who was found dead
in her high-rise apartment one Sunday morning. She had
died of "natural causes," so the report said. Yet in that apartment, police found ten cats, five parakeets, three dogs, and a
half dozen hamsters. The woman who had shown no sign of
emotional illness of any kind, who did her work well, who
seemed to "have it together," was, in fact, desperately lonely.
In all probability, the suggestion was made, she simply died
of loneliness—an inability to find on the human level satisfying relationships that would fill the void in her life.

Few people perhaps ever suffer the ravages of loneliness to
the extreme of taking to violence to compensate for it. Yet
far too many succumb to what that woman executive experi-

enced in being alone. Some lash out in their frustration and rage at not finding the answer to the emptiness in their lives. Others go on quietly, trying to "hold it together," seeking to find some measure of companionship that will suffice. Contemporary American culture has felt the sting of this "blue funk" perhaps more than any other. The 1970s have often been described by psychologists as the decade that ushered in an "epidemic of loneliness." A poll taken in Washington in 1974 proved the point, when 60 percent of the people questioned on the street admitted they were lonely "some of the time." The fact that so many people were willing even to admit to loneliness at all, when most try to ignore it or call it something else, is a fairly strong indication that this "secret killer" is on the loose as never before.

In *People* magazine (August 22, 1977) an interview with Dr. James J. Lynch, professor of psychology and scientific director of the psychosomatic clinic at the University of Maryland School of Medicine, made a strong connection between loneliness and illness. Lynch has pulled together his findings in a book *The Broken Heart: The Medical Consequences of Loneliness* (New York: Basic Books, 1977). When asked how close the connection is between loneliness and health, Lynch responded:

> That's like asking what is the connection between air and one's health. Like the air we breathe, human companionship is taken for granted until we are deprived of it. The fact is that social isolation, sudden loss of love and chronic loneliness are significant contributors to illness and premature death. Loneliness is not only pushing our culture to the breaking point, it is pushing our physical health to the breaking point.[1]

As to evidence in the linkup, Lynch added that the "effects of loneliness" are what takes the toll. "For example," he said, "the coronary death rate among widows between 25 and 34 is more than five times that for married women. The death rate for bachelors is 75 percent higher than that for married men, and for divorced men the death rate is more than double. Loneliness—isolation from others—takes a tremendous toll."[2]

Still most people, despite the evidence, will not admit to any problem with loneliness to that extent. They manage to keep going with it day after day, struggling in their private cells with this strange, smothering, constricting "blueness" that stubbornly refuses to yield. Some of these people—many of them—act normally, do well in their jobs, mingle with people without any sense of detachment and, by all the standards of normal behavior, "have it all together." But eventually the facades crumble. The empty apartment, the solitary meals days after day, the cold, empty bed, the haunting darkness of endless nights seem to inevitably wear away the composure. From there, if not relieved, depression moves in, and from then on the individual begins to slide under.

It is a strange paradox indeed that the most sociable people are very often the most lonely. The most successful, those at the top, suddenly for no apparent reason give up in their fight with loneliness and literally die. They may be walking around, be functional even, but they slowly lose contact with reality. Howard Hughes is probably the most recent example, among many. He spent his last years in a voluntary self-confinement, a victim of his own surrender to a private world that offered no solace for his needs.

George Sanders, the famous movie actor who took his own life in his Spanish villa, left a note that simply said, "I leave it all . . . it's all such a bore." For him, stardom, fame, and fortune apparently gave way to the weight of endless days of emptiness.

Loneliness is the most difficult feeling to define. Perhaps this is why it is so hard to treat. A man wakes up and hears a train whistle in the distance, and for some strange reason he begins to feel an "ache." After a while he senses this ache moving into a feeling of longing to go home or else to be on that train going somewhere to new things, new people, new adventures. But instead he soon realizes that he is in his bed, that he will probably never be able to make that train. And the feeling of being cut off from life moves in with a sense of finality, and he feels then only that heavy sense of aloneness. But if you ask him the next day to explain it that way, he won't, because he can't. All he knows is that for a brief moment in the middle of the night he had an "urge to travel."

Some women, long past childbearing, will hear a baby cry and shed tears. For them, though they can't explain the feeling, the baby is a symbol of youth long gone, of affections past, of age creeping in, of death ever so much nearer. For some, denied a child, the tears express their grief at never being able to be fulfilled as a mother. The experience is one of intense loneliness.

People go through all sorts of feelings in loneliness that again cannot be described. People in crowds, at concerts, even in church, will feel a pang of something that strikes to the heart and leaves them with a sense of drifting alone in a universe of uncaring people. For them, Samuel Taylor Coleridge's poem "The Rime of the Ancient Mariner" sums it up:

> Alone, alone, all, all alone,
> Alone on a wide, wide sea!
> And never a saint took pity on
> My soul in agony!

People in marriage relationships will sense "distance" at times from their spouses, often for no particular reason. A feeling of aloneness comes in when he will conclude "she does not understand me," or the wife will assume "he never really knows what it's like for me at home." If there is no open communication about these feelings, then the loneliness increases. Couples who move to separate beds often feel this aloneness more acutely, and the nights are spent listening to the clock chime the hours, while each is unable to understand what is going on inside himself.

Children feel detached from their parents often because of a lack of communication too, or understanding. Parents who openly refer to a son or a daughter as a "loner" do not understand how accurate and even dangerous that is. A child who is different by way of physical or mental power or limitation will feel this even more. Even those who are bright, get good grades, are active in school, and have friends will admit that home is "kind of a weird and cold place." They cannot explain their feelings adequately either—that it is loneliness. And because they cannot, or do not want to, parents presume all is well with them.

Some people, desperate to get out from under the grip of whatever this feeling is—again they won't confess that it is loneliness—will try their own remedies. So the fisherman talks to the fish; the farmer talks to the horses; the bachelor takes up a dialogue with the parakeet, and the favorites of all, of course, are the dog and cat.

One man took to talking to the paintings of Civil War generals in his study until after a while he could not separate the world of myth from reality. It proved to be embarrassing when he finally had company and kept asking, "General Beauregard, will you have coffee tonight?" Or, "General McClellan, is the soup to your liking?" The man was not yet mentally deranged, but he had carried on conversation so long with those famous figures that he could not negotiate the world of reality when it finally came to him. Fortunately, in his case, concerned friends surrounded him with their own real selves and led him out of his distorted, private world and restored him to normalcy.

But what is loneliness exactly? William Sadler, Jr., stated:

> In studying countless expressions of loneliness, both of modern Americans and from other times and places, I have found some common elements. The first and most outstanding feature of loneliness is a painful feeling, sometimes experienced as a sharp ache, as in moments of grief or separation; but it can also be a full, lingering form of stress that seems to tear a person down . . . loneliness also speaks of relationship, or rather the absence or weakness of a relationship . . . one can be lonely for another person, a group, a home, a homeland, a tradition, a type of activity and even a sense of meaning, or of God.[3]

Some state it to be a feeling of "disconnectedness" from the world, from people, from life in general. Harold Blake Walker in his book *To Conquer Loneliness* quoted Jean-Paul Sartre, who explained it this way: "We are isolated from others, from past and future, from meaning and value. We can count on nobody but ourselves, because we are alone, abandoned on earth, and without help. Life is absurd and love is impossible. So, we are condemned to futility in an impersonal world and in a universe with neither heart nor meaning."[4]

At the same time, whether definitions can clearly explain it or not, man has always had times of loneliness. No one ever goes through life without a period of "disconnection." Every age since the beginning has added to man's sense of aloneness in some way, but none has quite come up to the present.

There was a time when loneliness was accepted in terms of old people rocking away in a nursing home or a retirement farm in the barrenness of age in an uncaring world. Today it afflicts all ages, all classes, all professions with even greater intensity. And the ravages are felt more keenly.

The modern technological age has much to do with it, by putting man on an impersonal and expendable level. Man, who once felt that he was contributing something to his family and to his society by an honest day's work, now finds he is really not that critical to production. The computer has a brain capable of more accelerated calculation. People who are displaced in their jobs by machines lose their sense of self-worth. The welfare dole is hardly a cure-all for what ails them. A man, or a woman, must feel needed for what he or she can offer by way of some form of creative genius. If not, then purpose is lost; with this come loneliness, boredom, then depression, and finally crippling illness.

Aldous Huxley described these times as the era of "Fordism," a philosophy that demands we sacrifice the man to the machine and the mass. "People become things, and persons become merely productive symbols, with deadly effect on the creative arts, humanities, and the dignity of men. We are insiders in the sense that we are instruments of production and distribution, but we are outsiders when it comes to the personal relationships that stimulate communication and creative thinking."[5]

Symptomatic of the depersonalization of technology in the work role is the replacement of social intercourse by television. TV sets up a limited, one-way contact, however, while providing the glitter of reality. It deceives people into thinking there is communication, involvement, sharing, when in actuality it is simply a mechanized form of entertainment.

As Harold Blake Walker put it,

> Mass culture isolates man from society. We develop loyalties
> to brand names and TV programs, but we feel very little
> kinship to the nameless and faceless thousands who make our
> way of life possible. We are what Thorstein Veblen called
> "conspicuous consumers" of the products of our automated
> society, but we are underprivileged in our interpersonal re-
> lationships.[6]

The man who wound up talking back to his TV out of frustration in not being able to find an answer for his own social
need is understandable. He finally smashed it into bits in a
fit of anger one night. This only illustrates the extremes some
will go to in venting the futility they feel—that of trying to
find contact in this "one-way street." Few there are who recognize what is happening to them in their insulated "TV
lives," and fewer yet are willing to take the kind of action
necessary to free themselves from it. Destroying the TV did
not bring the man any closer to satisfying his need in terms
of fulfilling relationships with others than his months of false
dependency upon it did.

Apart from technology, of course, there are other factors
that contribute to loneliness. There are the status barriers
that prevent people from crossing over to each other. Eco-
nomic, intellectual, even religious sectarianism, all erect im-
penetrable walls to keep people out and in. People need people. When a person cannot find acceptance by others, when
there is little in terms of recognition for accomplishment,
when a person feels rejected either in romance, in peer-group
involvement, in clubs, or in the neighborhood coffee klatch,
that person loses something of self-worth. With that comes
loneliness, a feeling of being disconnected, of being cut off, of
being adrift, with nobody really caring.

The 1970s in particular have been called a whole new era of privatism. The head of the household looks after his main interest, which is his family. The battles for social justice and equality he leaves to someone else. He builds a higher fence around his yard, keeps his clan indoors at night, and pays as little attention as possible to his neighbors. Privatism is death in the end. To become deliberately disinvolved with mankind is but to invite loneliness to camp in the center of the family. What strikes home to that man and that family finally is that they have become:

> Alive but alone, belonging—where?
> Unattached as tumbleweeds.
>
> Author unknown

There is much to be said, then, for the Christian approach to loneliness. If loneliness is not forever, if, in fact, the cure for loneliness can be had here and now and not be put off until the hereafter, then it's important to recognize why.

For one thing, of course, the redemption Christ came to offer the world carried with it "reconnection" to God. Man is lonely mainly because he has been disconnected from the divine presence. But through Christ, as Paul put it, "All things are of God, who hath reconciled us to himself by Jesus Christ, and hath given to us the ministry of reconciliation; to wit, that God was in Christ, reconciling the world unto himself" (2 Corinthians 5:18-19).

The word *reconcile* simply means "to restore to friendship, harmony, or communion." When a person comes to know this reconcilation in Christ, then there is a fusion with God, whose presence can and does penetrate the shroud of loneliness.

This divine transaction is critical because the key to man's

loneliness is his inability (or even fear) to love. Ira J. Tanner
said, "We are lonely because of our fear of love."[7] In other
words, man basically fears love in terms of receiving it because of a fear of not being able to give it back in kind. When
a person cannot receive love, there is an ensuing loneliness.
In other instances, a person is afraid to give love because of
the possibility of rejection. If no love is given, the chances
are none comes back; thus, again, loneliness. Others, at the
same time, do not trust themselves or others in a loving situation—so they deliberately avoid intimacy, and in so doing
their inner selves weep. They slink away then and plunge
deeper into their lonely world.

What Christ's act of love accomplished on the cross was,
among other things, the restoration of man's desire, willingness, and *confidence* to love and receive love. "We love him,
because he first loved us" (1 John 4:19) appears to be a much
too capsulated statement, but it has sweeping effects upon
the man or woman who experiences that love that He showed
on the cross. For John went further to say, "Beloved, let us
love one another: for love is of God; and everyone that loveth
is born of God, and knoweth God" (1 John 4:7). Once the
fear of loving is broken by the love of God cascading through
a reticent heart, man no longer has to be afraid of being lonely
all his life.

But at the same time, lest there be assumed too sweeping
a promise in all the gospel transactions, Christians still can be
lonely. This does not cancel God's provision through Christ
at all, nor does it make a mockery of redemption. God never
intended that His own should retreat into a private, monastic
world, once having entered the bonds of fellowship with Him.
When He said in Genesis, "It is not good that the man should
be alone" (and He also meant woman), He recognized that

His own people are as much in need of companionship and fulfilling relationships as those outside.

The prophets gave vent to the loneliness that came by the very office they held—which was not always well received. Jeremiah lamented, "I sat not in the assembly of the mockers, nor rejoiced; I sat alone because of thy hand: for thou hast filled me with indignation" (Jeremiah 15:17).

Jesus went up alone to the mount of temptation and there battled the devil by Himself in that wilderness. He prayed His final prayer before His death away from any human consolation, in Gethsemane. His last great cry on the cross as the darkness of loneliness swept down upon Him was, "My God, my God, why hast thou forsaken me?" (Mark 15:34).

Paul charged, "All men forsook me" (2 Timothy 4:16) and at the end of his courageous journey for Christ spent his days alone in a dark, damp, and dreary prison.

Christians will have loneliness. The fact of it bothers many who actually do experience it, because they have come to believe that all negative human emotion is cancelled totally in regeneration. Christians will feel alone and lonely in their work, in their faith, in their churches, in their families at times, and suffer it as well in sickness and in separation from loved ones.

The missionary in the heart of the Amazon jungle has not had mail from home in months; though she goes on with her work unto God, the nights are long for her, and sometimes the days are heavy. The pastor, who is on demand to heal others, cannot find healing for himself. While he must dispel the loneliness of others, he cannot make known his own needs in this regard because the shepherd is supposed to be beyond the frailties of the sheep. The Christian worker who labors at the same task day after day without the benefit of some form of recognition will feel emptiness and purposelessness even though he or she is rendering service unto God.

The fact that one of the loneliest hours of the week for many Christians is Sunday morning in the local church is evidence enough that the Body of Christ does not fully grasp the needs of its own in this regard. And the bigger the "barn," as it were, the more anonymity and lostness people feel.

As one older woman put it, "I sit in the pew next to a warm body, but I draw no heat. I am in the same faith, but draw no act of love. I sing the same hymns with those next to me, but I hear only my own voice. When it is finished, I leave, as I came in, hungry for a touch of someone, someone to tell me I am a person worth something to them. Just a smile would do it perhaps, some gesture or sign that I am not a stranger."

The warning along these lines was sounded sharply by Paul Tournier when he said:

> It is the church alone, nevertheless, which can answer the world of today's tremendous thirst for community. Christ sent His disciples two by two. The great body of the early Christians, according to the Bible, "were of one heart and soul; they had all things in common" (Acts 4:32; 2:44). Instead of demonstrating the way to fellowship to the world today, the church seems to embody the triumph of individualism. The faithful sit side by side without even knowing each other; the elders gather in a little parliament with its parties and formalities; the pastors do their work without reference to one another.[8]

To the Christian who must grope on his own for some sense of attachment, there is the promise of Jesus Himself who said, "And I will pray the Father, and he shall give you another Comforter, that he may abide with you for ever" (John 14: 16).

But at the same time, John, writing in his first letter, said, "If we walk in the light, as he is in the light, we have fellowship one with another" (1 John 1:7). This means there is a responsibility encumbent on members of the Body to reach out to each other in light and draw toward one another in the bonds of love.

Loneliness is not forever. It need not dog the tracks of people in this life to the last dying breath. There is a way. The gift, of course, must be appropriated; but it must first be pursued. Some who have known liberation from loneliness must give of themselves to others still caught in their separate prisons. Some give, some take. But the takers soon become givers. This is the cycle of life in the Kingdom.

But the cure is conditioned on the knowledge of the malady. There must be honest admission of what loneliness is before the remedy can be found and applied. It is to this that every person must address himself or herself: *Am I lonely? Why? And then what must I do to conquer it?*

TWO

The Loneliness of Aloneness

In the tangled jungles of Indonesia, Sarah H. carried out a medical work among a headhunting tribe for seven years. She was alone all that time. The nearest station with any semblance of civilization was eighty miles away. Everything she needed in the way of supplies was flown in to her—sometimes that flight was no oftener than every two months.

Sarah H. stayed with her work day in, day out. Some days she never saw anyone. The headhunters were shy, withdrawn, suspicious. On those days (and there were often weeks at a time) she was shut in with herself—and with God. Other missionaries said she was tough. She was pioneer stock. Others called her a "spiritual giant," and she would have been all of these. Few, however, would even have given a second thought to the fact that Sarah H. got lonely. For her, perhaps, loneliness could be especially acute, because she was *alone.* She had no personal attachments. She dealt with hostility in her attempt to build bridges for God. There was no one on her level to whom she could talk. The language was still new, still not broken down. She had to try to communicate in gestures and with the few words available, which seemed entirely inadequate.

When Sarah H. was flown out of that wilderness in her eighth year of service, suffering an emotional breakdown, the news was baffling, even shocking, to the missionaries who knew her.

"Not Sarah!" they exclaimed. "Why, she's the last one to buckle!"

Sarah was only thirty-four years of age. She will recover from her collapse (because her fellow missionaries realized finally that there is room in the saint of God for human fallibility). It will take time, but in the end she will find herself, with God's compassionate help, and return to the frontier.

But the nagging question remains: Can a Christian, committed as Sarah was, become a victim of acute loneliness spawned by her aloneness? Obviously, yes. It does not mean that she was less spiritual because of it. The usual explanations that well-meaning friends throw out, of course, are "She lost touch with God" or "Maybe she really wasn't ready for it." These can be cruel and cutting words, though perhaps not intended to be. In actuality she did not lose touch with God, nor was it a case of "not being ready." She suffered the same frailty all humans do, over an extended period of isolation, and her being a devout Christian did not guarantee that she would be entirely free of it. Because she collapsed under the strain does not mean either that God was less toward her in His promises than to others.

Meanwhile, in California, Robert M. was rushed to an emergency room of the local hospital, complaining of chest pains. He was forty-two years old, a leader of an effective Christian organization working among businessmen of Los Angeles. He had never had heart trouble. But for three years, since he lost his wife, Robert M. had been alone. In those three years he fought to stay out of the webs of his loneliness. He worked harder, traveled more for the organization, sought to be active, and engaged in many social times, either on invitation or with himself as host. But for Robert M., as he put it, "It was the nights, those long corridors of hours, hearing

the clock tick, then chime—nights of darkness, of aloneness."
The fact that Robert M. had a heart attack was something
his friends would not attribute to loneliness.
"Working too hard, I always said," a neighbor of his commented.
"Wouldn't slow down," one of his fellow workers added.
Even Robert M. himself would not accept the fact that he
had driven himself to physical breakdown over his inner need,
the need for human, intimate attachment. Heart attacks are
connected with any number of emotional malfunctions, but
loneliness that drags on a man and pushes him to the limits
to compensate for it can be deadly.
Can this actually happen to Christians, even those committed and devout and seemingly "with it"? Can there be, as
Freud called it, a "separation anxiety" of aloneness that even
those in God can experience, sometimes to extremes?
Well, David himself substantiated this point, a man who
was the apple of God's eye, as it were, and yet, in one of his
many appeals out of loneliness, he cried out, "My days are
consumed like smoke, and my bones are burned as an hearth.
. . . I am like a pelican of the wilderness: I am like an owl of
the desert. I watch, and am as a sparrow alone upon the
house top" (Psalm 102:3, 6-7).
Elijah, in his prophetic role, seemed to feel the pressure of
his aloneness as he fought against the evil forces of his time.
It finally got to him when Jezebel sought to take his life; Elijah fled into the wilderness, finally sitting under a broom tree.
So depressed was he by it all that he asked God to be allowed
to die (1 Kings 19). Elijah didn't die; God reached him and
recommissioned him. But Elijah, nevertheless, knew what it
was like to stand alone in the gap and knew how the aloneness pushed him to the extreme of loneliness.

So it is certainly possible, and proved in many instances biblically and in contemporary experience, that a person can be in the heart of God's will and be lonely. Martin Luther lamented his lonely struggle as he pondered the great justi-fication passages in Scripture and pushed against the colossal might of the papacy in articulating them. In the same man-ner, a man or woman who determines to "lay it all out" for God against the prevailing winds of society is going to feel days of acute aloneness, which can bring loneliness.

There are all sorts of experiences and stations in life that produce this "separation anxiety," as it were. The death of a spouse, for instance, and the pain one can know by the ab-sence of someone close was described by the writer of Eccle-siastes when he said, "Again, if two lie together, then they have heat: but how can one be warm alone?" (Ecclesiastes 4:11).

Of course, the state of aloneness people experience in life does not necessarily mean crippling loneliness. Man is so made that, while he hungers for human intimacy on the one hand, there are times when he must be alone, free from the demands of human company on the other. Many times an individual needs to climb away from the traffic of life and be with God alone or just to allow his mind and emotions to re-settle. Aloneness, then, can be God's safety valve provided as a means to relieve the pressures of human demands. And there are those, too, who have come to accept their aloneness in life and make the best of it. They manage to push back the smothering arms of loneliness that leads to depression, and though their lot is an uneasy truce at best, they nevertheless have found the secret of coping.

But the issue here is in terms of those who suffer from aloneness they have not chosen to experience, or, in having it forced upon them, who must find some way to negotiate it lest it become a burden too heavy to bear.

It is encumbent upon the well-meaning people who have a world totally "together" in terms of human intimacy not to make hasty judgments about those who are caught in their aloneness. It is not enough to simply state, for instance, that a Christian's aloneness is due to sin (although that can be a reason), or that there is some personality quirk that keeps him or her forever in the shadows. To lump the saintliest of souls, the most dedicated and committed, in so simple a diagnosis is but to add insult to injury. It also denies one of the basic drives in man, Christian and non-Christian—the drive for human attachments, for acceptance, for love.

Perhaps the individuals who feel aloneness most acutely are those who are single or widowed. One is unattached and has no committed relationship with an intimate to fill the void; the other has known attachment but is now separated by death, as in Robert M.'s case. In most instances, the widowed have a more difficult struggle than the single.

Robert S. Weiss explained both situations this way: "There is a danger implicit in the situation of those who have never married, but it is even more threatening to those who have divorced and those who have been widowed. In the latter two situations there has been a loss of an emotional attachment; those who have never married have had opportunity to develop alternative arrangements, perhaps with parents, or with close friends."[1] Weiss adds that it is significant that unmarried women are presumed to be at risk of loneliness but not unmarried men. "Surveys to date," he says, "would suggest that loneliness is likely for each, but in our thinking we may continue to draw on the misleading but not yet discarded images of the lonely spinster and the carefree bachelor."[2]

The unattached female and male experience the same aloneness that leads to loneliness. Perhaps Sarah H. felt it more keenly against the barren landscape of a jungle outpost cut off from every possible familiar human attachment. And yet Robert M., in the middle of a busy, crowded life, could still feel the agony of it when alone. In any case, there certainly are no "carefree" bachelors or widowers, just as there are no "contented" spinsters or widows, in terms of the need for human intimacy.

However, too often the church, though not intending to, can complicate the aloneness that single people feel. For instance, too many in the church continue to play down the male in his singleness in terms of his need, while enshrining the female in her spinsterhood. The male who remains single "must have something wrong with him," or "He's just playing the field and enjoying it." This is a gross miscalculation. The female, on the other hand, is considered in her singleness to be "committed to God" and therefore to have turned her back on human relationships or intimacy for God's chosen place for her. This is assumed to mean being a missionary at an outpost, a director of Christian education perhaps, or a secretary in a Christian organization. The peculiar hallowing of the singleness of women by the church only increases their sense of aloneness.

Margaret L., a woman in her early thirties, is an excellent missionary teacher in Guatemala. She acknowledged her problem on this point, recalling, "Since I was twelve and won all the memory-verse marathons in the interchurch league, it seemed everyone slated me for some great missionary cause. They surrounded me with more halo power than I had, so much so that by the time I was seventeen I had not even dated yet. Guys in my high school classes, Christians, felt I was a kind of supersaint, a bit weird actually, a kind of untouchable, the Joan of Arc destined for a life of celibacy. I was labeled a kind of married-to-God-for-life person. I loved God and wanted to do His will, but that was not intended by Him to mean I was not to have normal intersexual contacts or even marriage maybe. By the time I was twenty-four, though, I had actually come to believe it myself, only because I knew by then that I was not going to have a romance like so-called normal people. I had this imposed heavenly aura over me. I don't blame God for that, but the people who insisted I was a 'rare saint' might have done me a disservice from the start."

In the same light, treating the male's singleness as simply a "phase he is going through, and he will surely meet a nice girl soon" is again pushing him further into his aloneness as well. He may not have his self-image together, so he may lack confidence and feel this does not attract girls. He may not have all the personality-plus or the virile handsomeness he feels is necessary to be comfortable around the opposite sex. What he needs in his aloneness is not more rationalizations for his not dating or marrying but a genuine understanding of his problem and some help concerning his withdrawal.

The church in its healing ministry must somehow reach these singles in terms of their aloneness and not simply rely on traditional, inadequate assumptions that celibacy is of God for them all. In other words, there is a lot more going on behind the single Christians' facade today than the well-meaning church member understands. Literally "canonizing" them on the one hand, or presuming there is something off-color in them on the other, is but to complicate their aloneness and bring on a deeper pall of loneliness.

Weiss adds,

> For the women who remain single through no choice of their

own, there are emotional crises to overcome. Realities have
to be faced, and the late thirties are likely to be a bad time,
especially in the life of a woman who may have to accept
that she may never marry and also that she will never bear
children. Some women can come to terms with these facts
and determine to make the best of it alone. Others lose self-
confidence, cease to care about their appearance, and may
grow rigid in their ideas and outlook. . . . For the older
woman social life can be limited or nonexistent; whether
single, widowed or divorced, she may find herself restricted
to an undiluted diet of female society.[3]

Men do not find it much easier, despite what people think
or presume. True, men control their world more, perhaps, and
since women still outnumber men, men do not feel so much
tension as women about the necessity of marriage earlier in
life. They can bide their time, or at least they think they can.
But the older a man gets, the less he feels he "has it together"
for marriage. He feels less capable of making the adjustment
to marriage and its responsibilities. His fear is that he may
become too set in his ways, too intractable for marriage. This
makes him feel uneasy, unsettled, and increasingly self-doubt-
ing about his own maleness.

Both the single female and the single male need help to
negotiate these inner fears and the sense of aloneness that
continues to pressure them. Church leadership could do much
to alleviate this, not just by more intersocial activities care-
fully chaperoned, but by a more adequate counseling that
will help singles find themselves and learn to relax in their
state of singleness.

At the same time, the "separation anxiety" that the widowed feel can, as illustrated by Robert M., become even more
intense. Having known the warmth and love of a spouse, life

is almost unbearable without a companion. In this case, loneliness is tied to a reaction to the *absence* of human intimacy that has been a part of life for many years.

Sometimes this total sense of loss and the encroaching emptiness of aloneness can drive some widowed people to extremes in order to compensate for it. Frank S. lost his wife to cancer after twenty-two years of marriage. He was at that time vice-president of a bank. He was always well dressed, mannerly, and immaculate about how he kept his yard, his car, his clothes. When his wife died, he seemed to lose his bearings. After a while, he began to show up at the office unshaven and looking haggard from lack of sleep, and his work began to suffer. He seldom went home, eating out mostly, wandering around town aimlessly, afraid to face the empty house. He did his best in church to relate, trying to "get it together" there, but he felt like a fifth wheel in couples' or singles' groups.

Desperate to correct his emotional state, Frank S. proposed marriage to another woman six months after his wife died. It was a hasty, almost panicky move to compensate for his loneliness. A year later his new wife left him, claiming Frank had tried to make her a reflection of his former wife. This often happens when a man marries too quickly after the loss of his wife. It didn't work in this case. After that break, Frank S. suffered a collapse. It would take him two years to gain restoration.

Well-meaning Christians advise people like Frank to get into a social group, mix a little to "get your mind off it." But Sadler warns:

> A person who sorely misses a special other person will not have that need satisfied by joining a group. Yet in spite of an impressive history of failure, we continue to encourage

widows (or widowers) to compensate by joining organizations. That is, we tell them to look to the social dimensions
to satisfy an interpersonal need. . . . If we recognize loneliness as a significant form of self-perception, consider its context and identify the dimensions involved, we will be better
prepared to face it realistically and positively.[4]

Of course, apart from marriage, other experiences can bring
aloneness and with it loneliness. There is social alienation, for
instance, when a person feels cut off or shut out from a group
he or she considers important. This can happen in the coffee
breaks in Christian organizations as much as anywhere else.
There are those inevitable cliques built around common acceptance levels of personality, intellect, or sociability. A person who is new to that organization and eager to experience
acceptance from others who have been there longer can suffer
a demolishing sense of alienation when not invited into the
various groups. The groups themselves may not be conscious
of what they are doing, nor do they intend to create an aura
of exclusiveness. But familiar patterns are hard to break.

Meanwhile, the person shut out will eventually take on an
antisocial air to compensate for what is experienced in the
way of rejection by others. Too often the groups responsible
go on in their own private circles, oblivious to what they are
doing to the person who feels shut out. For that person,
eventually, work performance suffers, self-esteem drops. The
feeling of being blackballed, exiled, or unaccepted, whether
or not such was intended, can do irreparable damage to the
emotional and spiritual balance of an individual.

Why should this happen at all within Christian cultural
groupings (and it does)? For one thing, some Christians are
prone to take for granted that other Christians "have it all
together." There is a false presumption that redemption

negates the need for human intimacy and fellowship with others, and that God is totally sufficient for what Harold Blake Walker calls the "inscape."[5] Even people in church, as illustrated earlier, can feel left out, simply because every one there presumes the same thing about the others.

For the person caught in this sense of aloneness within the sanctuary of the Body, it becomes more perplexing, because the Body is the one place where it should not be. Sensitivity is the rule, and if only one person in the group, in the church, or wherever is aware that someone else is hurting in this way—even though it may not show, because lonely people know how to cover—that person can become the key to the healing of the one feeling "outside."

Perhaps another dimension of loneliness that springs from aloneness is what a traveling man experiences far too often. Being away from home, from loved ones, locked into the bleak landscape of business on the road, causes sometimes the most acute pain. Joseph Bayly in his book *Psalms of My Life* summed up the feeling this way.

> I'm alone Lord
> alone
> a thousand miles from home.
> There's no one here who knows my name
> except the clerk
> and he spelled it wrong
> no one to eat dinner with
> laugh at my jokes
> listen to my gripes
> be happy with me about what happened today
> and say that's great.
> No one cares.
> There's just this lousy bed
> and slush in the street outside

between the buildings.
I feel sorry for myself
and I've plenty of reason
to.
Maybe I ought to say
I'm on top of it
praise the Lord
things are great
but they're not.
Tonight
it's all
gray slush.

But does it have to remain "gray slush"? Thank God it does not. There are those who face crises in their aloneness who manage to weather them and finally bring themselves together. They may have days of "gray slush" when they have longings for human attachments, for peer recognition, for acceptance. But they have managed to find in themselves, through God, a wealth of resources to keep them from being obsessed with their aloneness.

Harold Blake Walker explains the key to finding that sense of equilibrium.

Even though the landscape is lonely, the essential source of our aloneness is inside, not outside. . . . An empty mind turns inward and is bounded by itself. It is haunted by remembered hurts and anxious fears, swamped in the end by towering waves of self-pity. Its inscape is bleak and its horizon zero. The full mind turns outward to embrace the things of beauty that are a joy forever.

Through the centuries there have been men and women who endured isolation from the crowds because they were not isolated from the values that gave meaning to their aloneness. When Jesus approached the end of His life His disciples left Him and fled. He stood alone.[6]

And yet Christ had within Himself the values that gave him endurance and also a confidence in the resources of the Father to keep Him. He negotiated that desperate, dark hour of aloneness because of that.

Sarah H. knows now by her experience in Indonesia that she depended too much on the external landscape to keep her from being lonely. Part of the reason for that was simply that all of her Christian life had been lived within groups; she had never been conditioned to live apart from the familiar faces with familiar language and concerns. Her individual strengths were never tested, her ability to survive apart from others never really proved. Her external landscape, once it was stripped of that familiar contour, became a bleak one indeed. Perhaps her case on this point might be well taken by the church today, which puts excessive accent on interdependence and so little on the solitary walk with God.

Besides that, of course, Sarah H. has learned that her faith can open her eyes to a world around her filled with objects worth studying, examining, and enjoying—yes, even in her aloneness, and even perhaps because of her aloneness, she was in a position to have this experience. The longing for human attachment may always be there, but she knows now that until that is satisfied, or even if it is not, she has internal spiritual values that help her to look outward with the eagerness of a child looking on the world for the first time. These inner resources of her faith will never fail her, even if her road of service is a solitary one—*provided she uses them.* For her, a breakdown was God's way of helping her to realize this critical truth.

As Walker adds:

> Our capacity to cope with aloneness and to find meaning for
> our lives . . . depends on the aliveness of our minds, the in-
> tegrity and purposefulness of our hearts, and the faith that
> inhabits the inscapes we call our own. Faith is the "assur-
> ance of things hoped for, the conviction of things not seen."
> It is an awareness that the shadows of personal existence
> come and go against a background that holds together and
> is endlessly dependable. It is the conviction that God is in-
> volved with us all in our struggles to affect the growth of
> love and truth, beauty and goodness, justice and righteous-
> ness.[7]

Robert M. tried to compensate for his aloneness and loneliness by a frenzy of work and activity. Being active, of course,
helps, but to be driven by loneliness to the extremes, simply
to try to forget, is destructive.

What Robert M. needed to get hold of was what T. S. Eliot
said:

> You will have to live with these memories
>   and make them
> Into something new. Only by acceptance
> Of the past will you alter its meaning.

And there is a lot of truth in Axel Munthe's line: "A man can
stand a lot as long as he can stand himself." Sometimes it becomes necessary to turn around and face the enemy, as it were,
rather than run from him. Both Robert M. and Frank S. refused to do that. Their human frailty is understandable. Yet
confrontation with the issue of aloneness and "separation
anxiety" brings an admission of loneliness before God. Then,
as if a child had cried for light in the dark of night, God moves
in to relieve the loneliness.

When Jesus said to His disciples, "Peace I give unto you: not as the world giveth, give I unto you. Let not your heart be troubled, neither let it be afraid" (John 14:27), He was looking ahead to the time when they would feel loneliness and isolation in service. Earlier He had promised them "another Comforter, that he may abide with you forever; even the Spirit of truth; whom the world cannot receive, because it seeth him not, neither knoweth him: but ye know him; for he dwelleth with you, and shall be in you. I will not leave you comfortless" (John 14:16-18).

The word *peace* in the original means "wholeness," and that means as much the pulling together of a man's or a woman's "inscape" as anything else. Wholeness is healing for those who find themselves caught in the prison of aloneness that would eventually fragment them by loneliness and depression. Robert M. needed that "peace" in terms of wholeness within. Rather than allowing a part of him to remain adrift—that part of him that dominated all his thinking, that part of him that refused him rest—he needed simply to confess his loneliness and then draw on what Christ promised to give him. The same could be said for Frank S. in his need.

Margaret L. in Guatemala made her missionary work the focus of her life and managed finally to push back the sense of being deprived in terms of her need and expectancy for human intimacy. She blames no one now for her single state. She has found wholeness, or peace, within. That part of her that would demand resentment for her aloneness has been pushed aside by the anticipation of facing each day with a new realization—that she is fulfilling something of God in the lives of her Guatemalan students.

That does not mean she has abandoned her hopes for marriage, nor does she deliberately maintain a spinster careerist role over those hopes. But as she put it, "I am no longer anxious about it. I let God work it out either way. When I feel lonely, I let it come, but now I find something to do when it begins to work on me. Mostly though I let the Spirit do His healing within. He never fails to do so."

For those who feel socially alienated, or shut out from groups, there is no need to withdraw into a shell, to allow self-pity or even rage to take control. "It is the God-directed whose lives are anchored solidly in values that endure beyond time and tide and who are able to relate vitally to others," as Walker puts it. "Sometimes it simply means deliberately reaching out even to those who seemingly do not reach first. No one refuses a willing friendship deliberately; in fact, man is peculiarly constructed so that overtures of friendship are seized upon rather than turned aside. Only those emotionally ill can refuse such overtures."[8]

People who feel shut out from others perhaps might take note of the student to whom Sadler refers who said, "I am loneliest when I am out of touch with myself."[9] Sadler adds to this that "shyness, fear of loving and being loved, self-pity . . . are examples of traits that contribute to loneliness."[10]

When an individual faces the self aspect and determines first of all to know what the personal limitations for reaching out or being reached really are, that individual then is in a position to find healing for the "inscape." When that happens, there is less self-condemning, and he or she senses a greater willingness to make the first move toward others.

This does not mean that the group is free from the need to be more sensitive to those on the outer fringes. Some people just do not have the power to initiate gestures of friendship or produce acts of love. It is to these that mature Christians, who know what love and compassion and belonging mean, are to reach out the hand of acceptance and invitation. One who has "wholeness" is responsible to be the agent of healing in the same way to others. Those who "have it together" must work to help others find their completeness in God and in the Body as a whole.

Even then there is always the risk of rejection from the person to whom the gesture is made. Or the group may still refuse to acknowledge a person's desire for inclusion. But risk taking is what the love of Christ is all about. As Walker puts it, "We risk, then, the venture of love on the assumption that love, even for the unlovable, is better than hate. We hazard our lives on truth in the firm faith that integrity is more worthy than deceit. We risk compassion in the certainty that tenderness is wiser than cruelty."[11]

This is what the "ministry of reconciliation" must mean *within* the Body as well as without. To seek only to reconcile the world unto God, even as Paul pointed out, and then to leave people to negotiate their own course for human intimacy, is but to negate the true spirit of evangelism. Healing within in terms of providing intimacy for those feeling alone is necessary if the bringing of the lost, lonely souls outside Christ is to be made meaningful and not hypocritical.

Aloneness, then, need not lead to a perpetual aura of "gray slush." Aloneness can and does yield to the individual's will to see God standing in "the shadows, keeping watch above His own" (James Russell Lowell). It is within every Christian's birthright in Christ to draw on His presence through His Spirit, the Comforter. He never intended to replace human connection or human intimacy, but He can fill the voids, as He has done for millions who have turned to Him in simple faith. It is possible to wake up in the morning, separated from human attachment even, and face that day with a sense of promise that God delights to give. In the same way, it is also possible within Christian experience to lie down at night, turn off the light, and not feel the encroaching, smothering pressure of aloneness. Rather, though aloneness may be a fact, and it seeks to penetrate the atmosphere, God commands peace. And how many have known such an experience with the accompanying sweet oblivion of rest.

The hope in all this is expressed by Jeremy Seabrook in *Loneliness,* when he quoted from an article by Thomas Wolfe, "The Anatomy of Loneliness," which appeared in *Mercury Magazine,* October 1941.

> Then suddenly, one day, for no apparent reason, his faith and his belief in life will come back to him in a tidal flood. It will rise up in him with a jubilant and invincible power, bursting a window in the world's great wall and restoring everything to shapes and deathless brightness. Made miraculously whole and secure in himself, he will plunge once more into the triumphant labor of creation. All his old strength is his again; he knows what he knows, he is what he is, he has found what he has found. And he will say the truth that is in him, speak it even though the whole world deny it, affirm it though a million men cry out that it is false.[12]

It can and does happen just like that. The child of God ought to know it and experience it beyond his secular peer, for the vast resources for such experience in God are there. Aloneness is but a passing moment—or it can be a lifetime of hell. The individual alone, and his or her willingness and ability to reach out for those resources, is the key to what it shall be. When he or she does that, then the great accolade springs forth, "No, never alone, no, never alone!"

THREE

The Loneliness of Not Belonging

"How far are you going?"

"I dunno—far enough, I guess."

The truck driver half smiled. "That could be a long, long way." He glanced at the boy sitting next to him in the cab of the tractor-trailer. He could not be more than fifteen, looking even younger in the spaciousness of the cab, a little frail maybe in his worn Levis, tattered blue denim shirt, one small backpack held tightly in his lap. "Kind of tough at home, is it?" The boy did not answer. "Well—everybody comes to it some time. Some run from it. Then again some kind of turn and face it like a bullfighter facing the bull, right?"

The boy pressed his lips tighter as if he didn't want to talk about it. The truck driver waited. He had three sons of his own, so he knew. "Nothing to face," the boy finally said. "They got their own lives—I don't fit anymore. Maybe I never did. I got to find my own way."

"They tell you you don't fit?"

"They don't have to."

"Uh-huh." The truck driver felt uneasy. He had carried too many hitchhiking kids over the years, just like this one. They were more mature for their age in some ways than the previous generation, but in other ways they were still very young. Too young. Something had broken at home, that golden string that wound families together, and this one had spun off to find his own way. The truck driver was wise in not

41

pursuing it further. The boy would have to go to the end of the line himself. But the truck driver felt some sorrow as he realized that some didn't make it to the end of whatever journey they felt they had to have. Too many drifted into the cluttered corners of an unsympathetic world, victims of depraved minds, left mutilated by those who would use them for their own ends.

Meanwhile, as the miles lengthened between the boy and home, anxious parents would be spending hours on the phone, stringing together too many sleepless nights, turning over that haunting and condemning question "What did we do wrong?"

Perhaps not a thing. It is not committing a specific act of wrong that drives sons and daughters at times onto the road. They were good parents insofar as "good" means what parents think it means to children. They worked hard, they put bread on the table, built a home that had comfort, took an interest in their children's schooling and other activities. But the boy who moves out says, "I just didn't fit anymore."

Loneliness. All the normal patterns of a good family are there, all the elements of provision, all that would in a previous generation have constituted the "ideal." What had gone wrong?

"I didn't feel I belonged," one thirteen-year-old girl said, remembering her own "break out" and the wild ride that took her through a jungle of sex, drugs, and all the experiences the world offered as guarantees to put you "in." "My parents tried, but too hard. They talked about grades, looking nice, being acceptable as others expected. I had to be a good Christian, so they picked out those things they believed would put me into that right mold. I was reminded of them every day as long as I can remember. Sometimes I think they slipped it into my milk when I was two. All I felt was that they were expecting something of me that I owed them. What they wanted really was a proper Christian response for what they gave me, fed me, taught me. All I did was listen when they talked and keep my own mouth shut. If I opened it, I knew I was going to talk about things that didn't fit their ideas. When I did, they looked confused—then they went into polite silence. We just lost touch after a while."

This thirteen-year-old hit the road but was back at fifteen, sick, a girl now ten years older than her actual age. Most do come back, those who, like the prodigal, realize they had something far better at home after all. The loneliness of the road was far worse than what she had at home. "Maybe something of God got through in the end, but it was not a good reason for me to come home. I loved my parents; I missed them. But we are still lonely people here, though they are glad to see me home again. There is no answer to this, I guess."

Maybe there isn't, and yet maybe there is. Still there are too many who don't return. What makes them take such drastic steps to relieve their loneliness?

As Jean Rosenbaum, M.D., and Veryl Rosenbaum stated:

> One of the common causes of childhood loneliness is the feeling of being unloved and unwanted. It is true that this may be the result of misunderstanding or misinterpretation on the part of the child. He does not always understand the adult world and adult interests. Children are self-centered. It is only as they grow in emotional maturity that they are able to accept the fact that they cannot always be the center of attention. During childhood when they are so emotionally and physically dependent upon their parents and other adults, it is difficult for them to accept the fact that adults have interests and areas of life that do not include them.[1]

That throws some light on the problem, but still the fractures within the family unit go on. Somewhere beneath the facades of the child's going through the motions that satisfy for the moment the expectations of parents there is an inner chamber of torment seldom exposed. There is a feeling of wanting to be what "they [the parents] want" and yet wanting to be what "I feel." Because of this perhaps no generation has produced so many strangers under the same roof as this one; no generation has exhibited such an unholy desperation to "keep it together" as this one; and yet none has so demonstrated the agony of parents and children seeing it come apart. No generation has seen the shift from traditional values of authoritarian parenthood to the demand for independence on the part of children as has this one; and perhaps no generation has seen so many futile efforts at implanting spiritual resources to compensate for rebellion, indifference, and individualism among children quite like this one.

In all of this, it is also true that children have never hungered more for "belonging" in the truest sense of that term, whether it be in peer groups or at home, than at this hour. Group identification and belonging is hard to come by in elementary and high schools. Badges of acceptance are not easily earned. The brilliant student is not necessarily the popular one. The beautiful or handsome may find that "rites of passage" to acceptance are given no more readily to them than to the homely. Youth do not know what that "magic button" is that will help them belong. Athletes seem to have it the easiest, but who then is to account for the star football player, a senior in high school, who committed suicide out of "sheer loneliness"? For him, athletics was the one way to find acceptance at school and at home. And who is to account for the girl who became beauty queen at her high school but in her senior year quit altogether and ran off to a commune, associating with the dropouts of society?

And even closer to home, who is to account for the seventeen-year-old who in his church had become a key leader around whom the senior high group orbited—who then suddenly left it all to join a Texas oil rigging crew, never to go inside a church again for almost ten years?

Belonging. Somewhere in the hidden "inscape" is that cry that never is heard by parents, teachers, preachers, church leaders: "I want to be me!" Perhaps it was always there in generations past, but in this one for some reason there seems to be a greater demand that pushes the younger to desperate measures to achieve that self-image. It is not enough to tell them they can't always be exactly what they want to be at the expense of others. Such attempts do little if anything to check their insatiable pursuit of themselves.

Part of the reason for the pressure on youth today is the shift in culture values on larger scales that nibbles away at those closer to home. The Vietnam War left children who were born and grew up in the 1960s, carrying a heritage of a national defeat. The sense of national pride, or patriotism, and national causes were lost with it. The 1970s ushered in a time of retrenchment in America, a withdrawal from international causes; a new era of privatism took over nationally and in the home. People were content to look out for themselves and let social activism be the responsibility of someone else. The loss of legitimate causes to which one could look for the future crippled the adolescent's sense of idealism. Without an "ideal," there could be no real sense of a proper motivation emerging. The result was withdrawal.

Clark E. Moustakas in his book *Portraits of Loneliness and Love* comes close to what that inner scream is all about.

Alienated from his own self, the individual does not mean what he says and does not do what he believes and feels. He responds with surface or approved thoughts and uses devious and indirect ways. He learns to base his behavior on the standards of others.

Conformity to the expectations and demands of others and submissive obedience to rules and regulations are basic forms of alienation.*

Or, as Kierkegaard put it:

> For in the fact that he despaired
> of something
> he really despaired of himself,
> and now would be rid of himself . . .
> what is intolerable to him
> is that he cannot get rid of himself.[2]

That fifteen-year-old boy riding in that truck was trying to push aside that part of himself that would not emerge. He needed more than rules and regulations on his life; he could not abide them without a sense of emerging into something of value for himself. He had screamed long enough inside, not at anyone in particular, but those closest to him were his parents. He could not say they had done anything "wrong" to him; it was only in the frustration in not finding what was right for himself that he felt alienated and turned to the road to find himself on his own.

Perhaps Christian parents have suffered more from this alienation from their children than secular parents—if not more often, then certainly more intensely, since it is not "sup-

---

*From page 33 of the book *Portraits of Loneliness and Love* by Clark E. Moustakas. © 1974 by Clark E. Moustakas. Published by Prentice-Hall, Inc., Englewood Cliffs, N.J.

posed to happen to *my* kids." Parents who worked faithfully to give their children spiritual values in church and at home find it almost impossible to accept the fact that none of it has apparently worked to their expectations in their children. Yet that thirteen-year-old who ran away came home two years later as much because of the "pull of the Christian values that stuck with me all those miles" as because of the retreat from the horrors of the world's exploitation—which says at least that despite what seems to be a failure on the parents' part, something does, in fact, penetrate the seemingly indifferent or even rebellious child.

Christian parents, however, who are most conscious of giving to their children just about all they have of values and even material things, cannot understand why a child wants to break out. Christian parents take it more personally because it strikes at their careful efforts to provide; it strikes more at their faith, which they were careful to maintain; and it even strikes at their sureness in God who now seems to have ignored all of their loyalty to Him in this regard. It can be just as lonely a moment for parents as it is for children—something children seldom think about in their preoccupation with their own needs. Ultimately then they ask the familiar biblical question, "Who did sin, this [son or daughter], or [we] parents?" (John 9:2).

Some blame the church for the lack of more innovative programs to challenge their children. Too often this accusation is true. The church in too many cases remains only a "water hole" for people to gather around once or twice a week, repeating familiar phrases in hymns or prayers or preachments. Too many youth find that this familiarity of word and form does not bring them closer to a solution to their own inner tensions of not belonging, or "being out of it." They are gen-

erally more conscious of the world of school or society, which
they have to face every day, where everything is moving and
changing rapidly. There are no simple solutions to the stark
realities "out there"; they then either succumb to the pressures, or they withdraw.

What the church does not do, far too often, is consider what
kind of struggle youth are in. Spiritual truth is dispensed as
a kind of continual indoctrination. Youth for the most part
do not want indoctrination as much as experience. The experience they are looking for is that which will bring God
into their lives in such a way as to convince them that there
is a dimension of life worth living called Christian.

Of course, not all churches are guilty of missing the mark.
But those who have caught the level or needs of the young,
the loneliness in particular that is peculiar to them in this
generation, have found something of the secret to winning
these hearts and giving them a new surge of spiritual life and
meaning. Again it takes a conscious awareness of youth to
sense this. To continue to rest on form and presumption is
less work, but it is also less fruitful. Parents who sense the
church has failed their children in this regard may have a
point; it is for the church leadership to honestly review the
criticism and, if necessary, put its house in order.

But, of course, not every household experiences the fractures of children so lonely in not belonging that they take
desperate measures to break out. But then the question comes
down to, Why do some "have it together," and others do not?
Or, with that, What does it take to bring sons or daughters
into that glorious feeling of knowing they are what they are,
and, knowing that, into peace with themselves and with the
family as a whole? Suggested answers to these come later.

At the same time, the questions of "belonging or not belonging" are not confined to children. Husbands and wives may experience them with as much acuteness. The wife of a highly successful minister confessed that candidly when she said, "I am known only when I am with him. When people see me without him, it's as if they are seeing me for the first time. He is the axis of their lives; I merely come along when I can. I am not a piano player, a soloist, a typical Mrs. American Minister, a great and gifted teacher, or one who glows with the lights of all the heavenly galaxies. I cook his meals, bind up the wounds of his children, play hostess to the endless parsonage social events. When it is all over I retreat to my bedroom and sew; and then I feel forgotten, useless, disconnected, sometimes totally at sea. My faith holds me together, of course; my commission is to keep my husband in socks, underwear, clean shirts, and vitamins. I make him look as good as I can, keep up his morale, and provide him with the necessities of food, sex, and companionship. That is what my commission is, but that is not what I feel the church wants me to be. I am not sure that even my husband is content that I confine myself to the menial, even on his behalf. That is when I feel out of it, that I don't fit—and that's when I feel very lonely."

Or, again, consider the wife of a successful Christian businessman who must spend a great deal of time in conventions. "He knows everybody there," she confessed. "They are his world. They know him. When we get to a convention, he is gone, and I am left to fend for myself. I know none of them. Attempts to get to know them are awkward when I don't know the language, the nuances, the product called real estate. So I spend a lot of time in my hotel room, going shopping, sightseeing. But it's a drag. He tries—don't get me wrong. But he feels more responsible to his clientele than to me. So I finally gave up on going to conventions with him. But staying home only puts me farther outside his career, and a wife needs to have some part in her husband's dreams and accomplishments. So the loneliness gets heavier, the feeling of uselessness greater. I realize my need for him has to be given up at times for his success. But that doesn't change my loneliness, my sense of not belonging."

Sometimes it happens to husbands too. Some wives who have gone on to become successful in community affairs and in careers that put them in the public eye have left their husbands behind in the same way. One woman, a successful author, was married to an electronics engineer who designed TV circuits for a big manufacturer. Their worlds were distinctly different. The wife orbited in literary areas, something the man was totally unfamiliar with. The wife could not abide electronic technology. In her social events, the husband found a corner and stood out of the way, sipping his coffee by himself. Attempts at conversation were awkward since he could not come up with literary subjects or respond to any. Soon he stopped going to "her functions." Then he was home alone, watching baseball on TV, making his own way. The wedge had been driven between them, and the alienation was growing. Neither knew how to alter it. Soon he would find his outlet with the boys at bowling, hunting, or golfing. "My wife has her life, I have mine," he would say, but even as he said it, he knew it was not right.

But who hasn't felt that sense of not belonging? In spite of the best of intentions, even in Christian circles, it can happen. A man unschooled in the Bible may think of himself as at least an "odd ball" with the theologians; a woman who is not witty or "quick on the draw" may find herself feeling like a dunce among those who are "sharp on the uptake"; a man who is not highly intellectual may feel a crushing loneliness among those who discuss metaphysics or analyze "divine cosmology in the light of Francis Schaeffer or C. S. Lewis." Square people find themselves all too often trying to jam themselves into the graces of the round people. They won't fit. "Separation anxiety" emerges. And they wander off, find a place in an obscure corner, and keep company with a protective rubber plant.

Being a Christian does not always alter the state of one who may experience this feeling of "being out of it." That does not at all mean God is less to His own in this regard; it only proves that His own have not risen to His expectations in the area of human relationships. It takes disciplined awareness and sensitivity in the Spirit to detect in a social event one who is wandering around the room, touching here and there but never stopping, trying to "get in," but finally drifting off aimlessly, looking a bit terrified. That one cannot abide remaining in a corner in a crowded room forever, nervously gripping a drink until the knuckles are white.

Again, it takes a keen professor in a classroom to recognize those before him who cannot fit in. They sit withdrawn, unable to match the performance of the brilliant ones, those who seem to "have it all together." It takes great discipline and, again, sensitivity for such a professor to refuse to pander to the "quick on the draw" students, because they stroke his ego as a teacher, whereas the others do not. But those who are not "with it" nevertheless are saying to him, "You are not coming through." Their inner scream is simply, "You are too far beyond me—I cannot reach you, and you are not concerned in reaching me. You are sorting out the brains in this class from the slower thinkers; you are shutting me out in favor of those who mean more to you, who fill your loneliness.

But while you find in them reprieve, I find none for myself. I
don't ask for condescension but merely recognition. Tell me
I am worth something to you!"

Clark Moustakas summed up this loneliness of not belonging when he wrote:

> What has happened to us as human beings that we can be so
> near and yet so far, that we can be so distant from each other
> and not even know? Where are we anyway in those hours
> when the human spirit cries out in despair, when the hunger
> for sharing and for loving comes through in disguised and
> devious forms? What has happened when we have become
> so radically cut off from our own humanity that we kill the
> human need for compassion and understanding, when the
> longing for response is not even recognized or noticed?[3]

There are no simple or canned answers for those who feel
shut out, who sense they don't fit. But there is a spiritual
framework that can and does provide the necessary values
and attitudes. The Bible does not formulize specific answers
for every situation of loneliness. But it does focus on human
needs and the approaches to meet those needs. The danger
is in concluding that biblical truth, once used and faithfully
dispensed at one point in time, and having not produced expected results, cannot be applicable again. The Christian
must constantly reevaluate scriptural suggestion and command in terms of the changing circumstances. Human sensitivity is what the Bible teaches; the Bible is not something
simply to be memorized and defined in terms of house regulations. It is a Book relating how human understanding and
compassion, rooted in the heart of God, reclaims broken lives,
tormented souls—yes, lonely people.

For instance, in all the cases of loneliness brought on by
not belonging, there is a sense of failure hanging over the in-

dividual—the failure to be what others expect, the failure to relate properly, the failure to perform in such a way as to win acceptance. This is the most critical problem confronting youth, because society and the church continually emphasize levels of work and spirituality that make for success.

Nobody knows what John Mark felt when he was told he was through. He had failed. One can only deduce from what adolescents feel in like situations today that he knew emptiness, loss of self-image, the demolishment of dreams.

Perhaps Paul was right (Acts 15:37-40) in his judgment of Mark and in the penalty imposed. Perhaps Mark was out of his depth, perhaps he was too young, or was not capable of "cutting it" on a missionary trail that had death at every corner. Maybe Mark was not missionary material after all.

And there is a time, of course, when disqualifying an eager but careless youth is necessary to jolt him back to reality. There is a time when forgiveness won't correct chronic indolence—which was not necessarily Mark's problem and the Scriptures don't really say—but only the harsher treatment of refusal. But it is not always easy to know when to apply a harsher treatment or a more understanding one. Paul chose his way—he is to be respected for it.

However, sensitivity to the person involved is what makes the difference and determines the remedy. Barnabas did not agree with Paul's way. In fact, the two men had such a disagreement over it that they parted company. Today there is in many a household the same disagreement between parents as to the measure of "cure" needed for the child who has failed. Though they may not part company over it, the tension remains.

But what the young ask mostly is: "Just what is failure?" The diary of that fifteen-year-old boy riding in the cab of that truck gave some interesting insights into his frustration at not coming up to the standards set by his parents:

> Nothing is ever right . . . not good enough . . . seems I'm climbing a rope every day hand over hand . . . it keeps swinging on me, and I can't get a grip . . . and Dad keeps shouting up at me to use my legs, then my arms . . . you can make it, he keeps shouting . . . but I'm no rope climber . . . so I don't make it . . . he says we'll do it again tomorrow . . . why again tomorrow? What's so important about climbing his rope? I'm not cut out to be a preacher like him . . . or making A in English or math . . . I like to fix things . . . but that's not Dad's or Mom's rope to success . . . so I have to try climbing their way tomorrow . . . how do I tell them I'm not even a rope climber? God knows . . . but why won't He tell them?

Failure for the young then is not being able to climb the "rope" given to them by their parents—their parents' way of making it to the top, their own measurement of success. Much of that may be born out of good intention, but it does not take into consideration the inner scream of the child who is trying to say he or she does not want to go that way. "Sometimes," as one counselor put it, "a child will be pushed too far up that rope and will finally give up and hang himself with it. By hanging, I mean they cut out, they leave it, they run away."

Again, some of the young fail because their parents drive them up a rope they themselves will not climb. Inconsistency in terms of behavioral demand, the insistence on getting to the top in certain ways that they themselves do not practice, can frustrate the young even more. Preachments, compulsory church attendance, nagging about dress and manners or spirituality, which does not always measure up in them in like fashion, put the young into a quiet rage. Resentment builds until the inner chamber breaks under the pressure.

Barnabas could not agree that John Mark should have to climb the rope Paul had set for him for missionary service. Barnabas was looking at the future of this young zealot rather than at his present mistakes. Perhaps Paul was looking for a carbon copy of himself—the aggressive, brave, daring evangelist ready to run through the ring of fire for the sake of preaching the gospel. Barnabas, on the other hand, might have been looking at John Mark as one who was distinct, who had his own makeup, his own contribution to make in his own way, if not now, certainly later on. Paul had no time to spend on teaching Mark or giving him apprenticeship training. Barnabas, however, undoubtedly sensed that Mark was worth restoring for Christ. To do so cost him the greatest adventure with the greatest Christian pioneer of them all; but for Barnabas it was investment in a life, a life that had to go on when Paul and he himself left the scene.

In any case, it was Paul who recognized later the rightness of the approach of Barnabas when he wrote to Timothy and said, "Only Luke is with me. Take Mark, and bring him with thee: for he is profitable to me for the ministry" (2 Timothy 4:11).

What brings a young man from failure in one man's eyes to profit to that same man? What parent has not pondered the mystery of that? Somehow, somewhere, a concerned Barnabas refused to allow a young, sensitive, vulnerable youth to falter under the crushing load of not fitting in. Parents can and should play the "Barnabas" role. Sometimes, however, it is a camp counselor, a teacher, a preacher, a youth director—but when it happens, it is because someone has understood the need for sensitivity to youth who constantly feel unable to rise to the expectations set for them by the home, the church, or the school.

The "Barnabas" attitude is one of listening. Too much time perhaps is spent by churches and parents in inculcating the young against the drift into the world. Parents, in this role, become frustrated when it does not work, and they find themselves screaming, "Why don't you find something worthwhile to do?" (Climb the rope of success, *my* rope.) The question does not take into consideration the inner wounds that the question has inflicted on that child already. He or she doesn't know why either. What is "worthwhile"? He or she wants to scream back, "Where am I supposed to go? What am I supposed to do? Be like you or find my own way?" He or she does not know what his or her "own way" is but is struggling to find it. The child wants to share that, but a screaming parent won't allow it.

The "Barnabas" heart is the heart of God. It is a heart that *listens, loves,* and *understands.* Parents love their children but fail to recognize that love is not simply a hug or a kiss or a giving of things. Love is shown mostly in taking the time to create an atmosphere in which sons or daughters can feel comfortable in talking, expressing. If they cannot articulate their inner frustrations about themselves, to whom shall they go? All they can do is go on feeling "weird" in their inability to succeed, to climb someone else's "rope."

Now and then a wise high school teacher in a Sunday school class catches the genuine need of adolescents and throws out the book, as it were. Instead, he relates by opening the tender areas he knows compose that inner chamber of their lives. Instead of talking or teaching the lesson, he *listens.* One teacher did it with a mixed class and did not get through for two hours, so enwrapped were those high schoolers in opening up their inner torments to him.

"Why can't you get it together like your brother or sister?"

is another cutting question a parent may ask. This is not the "Barnabas" approach. This attitude does not view each person as distinct, as created by God to be different, and thus to find his or her own way. As Martin Buber put it:

> Every person born into this world represents something new, something that never existed before, something original and unique. It is the duty of every person . . . to know . . . and there has never been anyone like him in the world, for if there had been anyone like him, there would have been no need for him to be in the world. Every single man is a new thing in the world and is called upon to fulfill his particularity in the world.[4]

The creative genius of God is not confined to making carbon copies of parents or missionaries or preachers or anyone else deliberately shoved up on the horizon as the model. Youth today are not interested in being molded into the forms of accepted church vocations; but they are interested in knowing how Jesus fits into their hours of lonely struggle even as they want to know how they fit into His concern for them.

The father who, even with good intentions, creates problems for his son or daughter may say, "You don't need to feel out of it. You are capable of being an 'A' student. You can do it if you want to. I did it with less opportunity than you. But it's really up to you. If you want to sulk about it, be indifferent, then it's up to you. You might try praying a little about it too and more reading of your Bible."

There is no *authenticity* here. It is the pep-talk approach, the digging at the already lacerated wounds within. But the "Barnabas" father who is being authentic would put it this way: "So you lost today. You may lose tomorrow. I lost a few myself today. Life is made up of a lot of losses before

you win one. Sometimes I get mad about it. I want to kick
the dog when I come home. Then I just want to go off somewhere and get away from everybody, you, everybody here.
But then I figure that's a cop-out. So I realize the Lord
didn't make it in his hometown of Nazareth either—He went
there twice, and both times they gave Him a lousy time of it—
even tried to toss him off a cliff once. So I say to myself: Well,
then, that didn't stop Him. So I guess it won't stop me from
getting up tomorrow again and facing the same big wide
world, win or lose. I don't mind losing, see, if I learned something about myself—that's what it's all about, and since we are
having to learn the hard way many times, then there has to
be a lot of missing the mark now and then before we win."

Again, the teacher who will play the "Barnabas" role and
see in every one of his students someone unique, distinct, a
person with potential to do well, will recognize there is loneliness there that may prevent the student from attaining. The
professor who is sensitive to those who are slower, more reticent in class, more uncertain, and more lonely, will be careful
in how he approaches them.

The professor who sits behind his desk to talk to these "out
of it" students is threatening to them. Desks are official-look-
ing instruments that represent the institutional image. The
desk poses an atmosphere of a counselor to an emotionally
sick patient. It breathes of legality like a lawyer getting ready
to provide options, a doctor ready to discuss the X-ray. A student who is lonely because he senses he doesn't belong with
the "brains" in the class is hanging on the edge of failure. He
needs intimacy—he needs someone to listen, to take off the
legal, frightening garb of professor-student relationships. He
or she right then needs the human touch, a relationship based
on human and divine values of concern and not on grades or

class performances.

The professor needs to come from behind that desk, take that student to the coffee shop—change the environment—and in so doing provide the atmosphere for honest and genuine interchange. Too many teachers avoid this. To take the desk away from them is to take away their prop, their position of authority. But for the lonely student, made more lonely by the sense of failure hanging over him, when a professor senses this problem and then seeks to become *authentic* as a listener—getting out from behind that desk—the student does not feel as lonely. A sense of rapport emerges, a sense of concern on the part of the professor that says, "I *am* interested in you as a person."

When the professor speaks from behind his desk, he may sound this way: "You have the same opportunity and potential to make this course as anyone else. It takes harder work, longer hours, but that's what education is all about. Your responsibility to God is to work harder. You owe it to Him and this school. Others are making it; I have confidence you will too."

All he needs to do at the end is to pound the gavel and say, "Next case!" What he has done is to drive that lonely, frightened student deeper into his terror, uncertainty, and urge to run.

But the "Barnabas" professor gets out from behind the desk and after his second cup of coffee with the student says, "I feel you are not with me in class, and maybe I understand why. Some of this course load is heavy, some of it won't get through except to minds completely honed to the subject. I failed Economics 101 my first year at university, and I almost dropped out. *Nobody* fails Econ 101, I was told. But I don't have a mathematical mind. The professor was a genius.

So where did that put me? He was three weeks ahead of me all quarter. I got left in the dust. I don't want you in the dust. I want you with me at the end of the quarter. So I'm going to help you all I can. You are more to me, see, than a name on a roll sheet. OK?"

The confession of doubts from the teacher, the honest desire to share with the student, lonely in his sense of failure, is a demonstration of authenticity. The student now feels he or she can talk about the inner frustration, the pain, the lostness. Now there can be healing, the reconstruction of shaky pillars, the reinforcing of mental powers, the reminder of spiritual resources, and the love of God building bridges between professor and student.

It happens. For those who catch the biblical appeal to sensitivity as Barnabas had it, it does happen.

Is it any different for the others who experience the loneliness of not belonging? If the minister would take time to realize his wife's feeling of not fitting in as a pastor's ideal wife and would talk more with her about his need for what she can do well, would that not cut the shadows of failure hanging over her? The minister who says to his wife, "I love you for what you do to make me what I am. You keep my home, you care for the children, you support me in prayer. I love you just the way you are—and I am proud God gave me a wife who does so well what God has given her to do." Whether or not the church congregation agrees with him, a minister who conveys that to his wife is giving to her a confidence that relieves her loneliness and makes her feel a real part of him, a needed part. And the congregation that will accept her for that role will know in her a treasure as well, because in that mundane ministry of hers, she is contributing to the ongoing strength of its pastor.

Would not that husband who went off to conventions, leaving his wife behind, do more for her by practicing the biblical value of sensitivity and taking the time to draw her into his career rather than shutting her out? Many a businessman in similar situations—yes, even many an evangelist—has deliberately taken the time to explain his work and then seen to it that she was with him on as many conventions or campaigns as possible. A wife shunted off to shop, to sit in a motel room, or to stay home is right to assume she does not complement him enough. Maybe the man does not intend that, and there are times when she cannot be with him. But when he deliberately seeks to involve her with him, there is a change in her own self-image, which is more than simply extra baggage for his life.

For the career wife who considered only her own literary clique at the expense of her TV engineer husband, would not the biblical value "loving one another" have led her to share an evening or two with his friends from the shop even as she demanded that he share evenings wth hers? Would not the wife be practicing and fulfilling the "Barnabas" sensitivity by watching TV with him some evenings and listening to some of his experiences in TV engineering? Would there not then be built into her husband a new sense of interest in her career, and would he not then feel less loneliness in having to find reprieve with men from his business to the exclusion of the one he loves? It all depends on the willingness of individuals to recognize the needs of one another in the Christian framework, if this is to occur.

Any individual, then, in the Body of Christ—and consider the many, many of those outside Christ who find themselves in Christian social events—who feels "out of it" for whatever reason needs the ministry of those who are spiritually sensitive to loneliness in others. No one should have to feel less in value than anyone else in the Body of Christ because of job, education, personality, or position. If the Son of God could wash His disciples' feet as an act of service to His own, is it too much to ask a hostess to be sensitive to those terrified souls who seem to be shut out from the intercourse of fellowship?

Authentic Christianity is articulated in the sensitivity of Christ's own, be they parents, teachers, whatever, to listen, to love, to understand. It is also articulated in the Scriptures: "For he that is least among you all, the same shall be great" (Luke 9:48). Those who sense in others a lack of feeling important to anyone else, and who then provide the mantle for them to be accepted for who they are, are in fact fulfilling a great service to God and to man.

At the same time, for the young who run away from home to relieve their frustration and loneliness, there is as much need to realize what they have done to inflict painful loneliness on parents. The young have come to assume that loneliness is a disease; they have concluded that they can live apart from parents, ignore them, and cultivate their own journeys apart from those who love them and are concerned for them. The young who in their inner agonies of conscious failure take drastic steps in running away do inflict punishment on parents. If there is godly sensitivity at all in that young life, then he or she would do well to think twice before uprooting the home with selfish drives to prove something on his own.

That thirteen-year-old who returned after two years is now a junior in high school. "I realize now how much my running off cost my parents. They are older, older than they should be. I can see the pain yet in their eyes. They are changed now. They listen more. Even to what I have to say about small stuff that goes on in school. Sometimes we can still laugh too, but I regret having run away just to prove something to myself, to find some meaning for myself. I think the cost for them was not worth it. I have asked their forgiveness for running. They have assured me it is all right, that it is behind. But I gave them a long two years of loneliness and tears. I think we all know that maybe I had to make that journey. But then again there has to be a better way, a way that does not rob them or me of so much in time and love. What we have now is important. There is nothing like being home where everyone listens to each other—no one is screaming. I could wish it for every parent and every kid in every house. Running does not help, and it should not be the only means to get peace—there ought to be a way to work it out together, to say what we feel and think without feeling put down. Otherwise, the other way—running—leaves only scars that never go away."

But that fifteen-year-old boy is still traveling. Some day he will come home too—it is hoped. God wants him home. Parents want him home. And maybe the only assurance to be had for parents is in what Jesus said in response to the question, "Who did sin, this man, or his parents, that he was born blind? Jesus answered, Neither hath this man sinned, nor his parents: but that the works of God should be made manifest in him" (John 9:2-3).

Sometimes a child must make that journey by himself or herself. Again, it is not for the parents to take on crippling guilt over the possible mistakes made. Someone, by God's sovereignty, will become a "Barnabas" to that wayward one and help him to find himself again. Sometimes the young can "get it together" only through the help of someone outside the home or the church. The bright young man who ran off to a Texas oil rig had to have that experience. He lived eight years away from home and church until a Navajo Indian Christian helped him to know about himself. It took ten years to find what he needed, but today he is in church again, is now an oil business executive, and spends weekends with his parents. God can take the drastic, desperate moves of those who are lonely and lead them to that necessary confrontation with themselves.

But while they are gone, their hearts are never far from home. For whatever mistakes of others or own sense of failure drove them out, love is the golden cord that is never really broken. That is why many come home again—why some eventually find their way back.

And when they do come home, they know "belonging" as never before, because in their search for themselves they have come to know the winter of lostness. It is God's way of showing them their true roots and that, no matter how far out they go, sooner or later they must return.

But what of those who have not yet left? What of the wives or husbands who stoically endure the long hours away from those they love for whatever reasons? Or those who have come to experience marital distance and are desperately trying to hang on, to ignore their sense of not belonging, and are hungrily yearning for some way to fit in?

To these situations Paul said in Hebrews, "Let us consider one another to provoke unto love and to good works" (Hebrews 10:24).

There is still time to mend broken fences, to "provoke unto love," to reach out and touch in genuine love. There is time to begin listening, to catch the pulse of those frightened by their loneliness. There is still time to heal, time to build, time to give others a sense of value as God-given.

There is still time to reach out to each other and say, "You belong to me! I need you!"

FOUR

The Loneliness of Broken Dreams

She knew now she would never write a novel.

After eleven years of struggling at the typewriter, Claire realized that all the starts and stops of putting together a piece of literature were not to materialize for her. A successful teacher of retarded children, she had written many articles on the subject for education journals. But her dream had always been to write the novel she knew "was in me."

But after five publishers rejected it, and when a publisher, a close friend, told her as kindly as he could that the novel was beyond her calling, she knew then. She did not "have the gift of words or the dramatic flair to produce this form of art." Period. The realization was staggering to her. For years, others had encouraged her, though they were mostly struggling writers like herself. Ministers, who had compassion but little insight into the necessary gifts and qualifications for novel writing, urged her to "write the vision," and, "God will honor your effort in the end."

But now she knew for a certainty that it had come to an end. She was older now; there was no longer the energy she needed to keep at the project that had consumed her for so long. The manuscript had been reworked more than twenty times. She had been through agents who took her money, gave her canned advice, but never offered to try to get her work published. She had attended night classes at the university to perfect her style, had taken in dozens of writers' conferences, had even hired a fiction writer to help her over the "rough" spots.

But now it was done. Her greatest moment of courage had to come now when she tearfully put the 360-page manuscript away for good. She could have gone on with it anyway, still tried, but she knew inwardly that the publisher who had criticized her so gently was right.

Now that she was truly aware that she hadn't a hope, the crush of it was almost too much to bear. With that came the loneliness and the days of depression. The familiar notes and pages that had always covered her desk were gone. Facing a clean, bare desk each evening or morning was a symbol now of death itself to her, of someone having died in the family, never to be recalled. Prayer stuck in her throat, mingling with her tears. When she became ill with pneumonia and was near death, she had not the will to fight. To recover meant climbing that mountain of life again without the anticipation of experiencing the one fulfillment she had worked for, so hard and long. Somehow, as much as she knew it was wrong, death seemed not so bad a solution.

What Claire experienced was not so much the loneliness of failure as that which came from unrealized expectations. She was already a successful educator and writer of articles on education. Even having missed the mark with a novel did not make her a failure in the fullest sense, like those who put all their lives, job, time, and money on a project and fail. For them failure is the total experience. But for Claire, as in the case of so many others, it was the demolishment of not realizing a secret dream, an expectation that was perhaps something carried over from a childhood fantasy.

The same kind of experience struck a young minister, Jim Q., who at thirty-nine years of age, at the peak of his pro-

fession, was informed that he was not going to be the new
pastor of one of the largest churches in southern California.
A gifted speaker, well-educated, dedicated, Jim took the news
without a word. But then he retreated into his study and allowed "something to die in me."

"I had built five churches from scratch in my eighteen years
in the ministry," he confessed, remembering his feelings of
the day. "I had fought those battles of starting out with a
handful of faithfuls and guiding them through all kinds of
hassles, living on practically nothing, but always keeping the
future ahead of me. One day God would honor my commitment with a church where I could have influence for Him in a
much broader sphere. I promised my wife who faithfully
stayed by my side, doing without so many things, and even
my children who had hand-me-down clothes and could not
look to college with the same confidence as others in their
classes—God would honor us. Then it came—the church with
over twelve hundred members in a key city, an influential
church without doubt, a church that I had always set my
heart on. To get that church would be a seal from God.

"Well—when I didn't get it, I figured what else was there?
Back to the little country churches? Back to starting churches
from scratch again? I argued a long time with God about
that, and it took a long time for me to repent. I am not sure
the bitterness is out of me yet. When you know you have
the gifts, the calling, the ability, when people in that big
church said they liked me, wanted me, and then you don't
get it—well, you feel abandoned by God, by people—you feel
more alone, even empty—I guess I felt I had it coming to me—
doesn't a man deserve to move up in the Kingdom of God just
as others do in General Motors or in any other business?"

Again, with Jim it was a case of unrealized expectations. It was not failure as a minister as such; he could always minister; there would always be a church for him; it was simply that the church he had set his heart on as "part of my calling" did not materialize. At the point of disappointment, even as in Claire's case, a person becomes highly vulnerable. Loneliness spawned by unrealized expectations can become a crippler, because any individual, especially a Christian who has come to expect God to work to fulfill the dreams, who finds that the ideal is out of reach, often experiences a slash in motivation about life and purpose. There begins for him a hopeless and debilitating round of questions about self-image, then a problem of self-acceptance, all of which force a person to withdrawal, bitterness, cynicism, and sometimes complete immobilization.

He or she then feels as Thomas Wolfe put it: "And then it seems to him that his life has come to nothing, that he is ruined, lost, and broken past redemption, and that morning— bright, shining morning, with its promise of new beginnings— will never come upon the earth again as it did once."[1]

Sometimes the pain of unrealized expectation hits at the very heart of what one considers *natural expectation* in life. For instance, Jane D., at thirty-six years of age, was told by her doctor that she would have to have a hysterectomy, that child-bearing was out of the question for her. Still single, yet attractive, and successful in a career as dental hygienist, she was looking forward to falling in love, marrying, and raising a family. She had given herself to her career, which she loved, perhaps too long; she had been dated, courted, proposed to. But she had put it off, because she felt her training deserved some time to practice what she had learned in her profession. Now she knew she had waited far too long, because now it was too late.

"I cried," she said, "in that doctor's office, and I was still crying when I went home. The doctor told me I could still marry and have a normal married life. But what is normal? Do I fall in love with a man and then tell him that I can't bear his children? How many men are there around who would accept that?"

Of course, there were men who would love Jane for what she was, and there was always adoption. But that is never the same for a woman. At least it wasn't for Jane. The hopelessness of her situation plunged her into a "blue world" that affected her work and her friendships. She became withdrawn, avoiding social contacts, except for church services. In six months she appeared haggard; she was not sleeping well. She was not eating either. Times of tears were too often, and she took on an unfeeling attitude about life. "I almost felt I was dead," she said.

For Jane, loneliness was not due to failure on her part. She had expectations that were normal for a young, attractive woman. Those expectations were suddenly demolished. She was helpless to account for it either in herself or in God.

Again, it is one thing to make an attempt in a job and fail; that has its own peculiar form of "separation anxiety." But it is quite another to mentally and emotionally condition oneself to expect certain things to occur, which are not really beyond possibility, and find that they are maddeningly pulled out of reach. Parents, as referred to earlier, expect their children to turn out to be model, and is this beyond expectation if all the family environment is properly put together? If there is spiritual and moral instruction—and a consistency in demonstrating it—should not there be an expectancy of seeing children rise up and call them blessed? Children may find their parents do not come up to expected measures with regard to understanding them or being willing to listen to them. Does this not likewise breed frustration from an unrealized expectation?

Whether in parent or child, unrealized expectation is a disappointment that cuts deeply into the soul. It breeds a nagging, ever-present ache in the "inscape." Sometimes, if it is allowed to stand, parents may blame each other for the unattained goal, and then, as in some cases, a serious fracture can occur.

In many cases of unrealized expectation, the intensity of it can be compensated for, because there is always an element of hope that the situation will remedy itself. Claire still had her educational career; the minister had a church he could pastor—many churches—even if he didn't get the twelve-hundred-member one; Jane could still meet a man who would marry her for herself and not worry about children; parents can hope and pray that the wayward child will still "shape up." But there are other cases of frustrated expectation that are almost totally demolishing.

For instance, a former POW in Vietnam, after seven years of imprisonment, had come to look forward with great expectation to the reunion with his wife and three children. Somehow they had managed to communicate with each other through the difficult Vietnamese prison system. When he finally returned home—the one dream he had that kept him alive through those long years—he found that his wife had married someone else. She told him, "I made a choice based on the percentages that said you would not get out alive. After all, I had to think of the children."

As that POW put it, "Life ended for me. I had taken everything the Vietnamese could do to me, endured the pain, the loneliness, the depression, the moments of near death, because I had my family in front of me all the time. I had prayed that God would see me through for them. Then to get that news, to see it all go up in smoke, I wound up in a mental ward for eighteen months. It was simply too much for me. I was not strong enough to take it, that's all. When I was released from the hospital, I was never the same man again, and I probably won't be. My faith in God had taken an awful beating. My faith in my fellow man, the moral codes, ethics, all seemed a mockery. I could not find my way back. I had a good job, but it was just to make money to make ends meet —I found myself hating the nights and even hating to get up in the mornings. I had nothing to shoot for; I was afraid to work for anything, to hope for anything, to expect anything."

Every individual experiences the pain of unrealized expectations. No man or woman can go through life without disappointment. Of course, there are many every day that are small, that can be absorbed as part of life. But the critical areas, for the Christian especially, are those that form the axis of life, the "reason for living." These constitute shocks that crack the human spirit, that drop a pall of emptiness over the soul. When terminal illness strikes the very young, or when it hits at the peak of a man's or a woman's working years, when life is giving satisfying rewards, then comes the devastation of loss and the accompanying loneliness.

It is this loneliness of unrealized expectation that is the real illness to be faced. It is a loneliness that says to a man or woman, "You are not good enough. You have never been good enough. You are not like other people who have it together, who win, who achieve, who realize their dreams. There is something wrong inside you. You are out of step with the human race. You will always be a loser. You will never attain your goals." And so it goes, on and on, until a

man or a woman comes to believe it and sinks lower into loneliness and despair.

Individuals who allow themselves to sink into the mire
that unrealized expectation precipitates usually react in several ways.

First, they may look upon themselves with self-pity. Why
does it have to happen to *me?* Christians can often allow this
to creep up on them, because they have been drilled in the
idea that once one is a Christian, God is bound to fulfill every
expectation. This is too often preached by evangelists or over-
eager ministers who wish to make converts. Christianity is
too often sold as the invitation to a Disneyland fantasy world.
"Security, safety, and enjoyment" is too often the slogan that
beguiles, and this sets up God as a kindly grandfather ready to
unload all the glories, wonders, and treasures of life that could
not be attained prior to conversion. The blow of unrealized
expectation in critical areas leaves the Christian wallowing in
self-pity perhaps more than those not Christian. It is a case
of saying, "God does not really love me, or He wouldn't put
me through this!"

Job is a classic example of self-pity as he responded to the
total loss of his family and possessions by sitting on an ash
heap and bewailing what God had done to him. A spirit of
self-pity leads to surrounding oneself with those who will rationalize the unrealized expectation in many ways. Not all of
that is bad, of course, because a person plunged into the confusion of being denied what appeared to be within reach
needs something to grab on to.

But in Job's case, his friends counseled him in terms of
where he had *failed* God—their rationalizations were in terms
of what he had done wrong. This kind of rationalization only
compounds the feeling of self-pity. This leads only to an end-

less round of introspection that becomes morbid. Loneliness then becomes complicated by self-recrimination.

It was not that Job had failed God at all, but rather that he should in his loss see God far beyond his human expectations. Who hasn't had a whole new awareness of the greatness of God only after the flimsy human dimensions of attainment have been pulled out of reach? It is not a case of God's playing cat-and-mouse with His own. Very often it is His way of getting the attention of those who cannot see Him behind the barriers of human attainments.

Rationalizing the unrealized expectation in terms of failure is dangerous. It adds to the self-pity rather than relieves it and makes God out to be monstrous in dealing with His own.

If self-pity is not faced and dealt with, then of course the next step is resentment. Now the individual becomes angry, rebellious. Unable to cope with the loneliness of what appears to be a rejection by God, the individual takes to reprisal against God. It now becomes a case of "getting even"; some refuse to serve in church work or maintain a calling that did not gain for them what they secretly anticipated. This becomes a toxin in the spirit that leads to bitterness and then cynicism. The individual is no longer content simply to lick his wounds in private; now he insists that others around him experience his loneliness, his sense of loss. His resentment must be shared by them. Even his reprisal against God must also be matched by theirs. The resentful person then begins to drag down others with him, even those he does not really want to hurt. Too many families have suffered from this kind of person in the house, this one who, as a pouting child, now inflicts his pain on them. Their lives take on a cloud of confusion and unhappiness, and the tensions build to explosive levels.

Besides the self-pity, resentment, and sense of reprisal a person may experience or allow himself to imbibe as a part of unhealthy reaction to unrealized expectation, there is also denial. Now the individual tries to convince himself and others around him that there never was a dream in the first place. This is self-deception. It is an attempt to compensate for missing out. The individual manages to keep up a good front; he even forces himself to declare, "I was never really serious about it anyway," and thus lets everyone know it doesn't mean a "hill of beans" one way or the other This person is desperate to avoid any possible conclusion by anyone that he has failed, even when he knows it is not failure that accounts for his not achieving his dream.

Denial does not change the person within; it does not alter the feeling of loneliness; it does not change the feeling of rejection or the frustration of missing out. It may seem the courageous thing to do, certainly better than self-pity or resentment, but in reality it complicates the inner emotions. The individual is being untrue to himself and to others. By his unwillingness to state clearly his disappointment, that he missed out on something he had his heart set on, he is creating dishonesty about himself. Then he becomes more resentful in having to deny it—so the complication continues.

A man who wanted to move to a newer and larger home for his wife and family was elated to get clearance to buy from the mortgage company. But he had to sell his own home first for the contract to go through. Meanwhile, while they were waiting to sell, he and his wife and family would drive around the new home every weekend and dream about what it could mean once they got in. Months went by, and the man's house did not sell. Realtors could not explain it. Even dropping the price did not bring a buyer. The contract time passed. The man's dream house vanished. The shock and disappointment struck hard at everyone in the family. The man, however, said, "Well, I didn't think it was for us anyway. Who wants such a big house? Just a lot of maintenance—maybe there are more flaws in it than we think. I'm glad we didn't get it— really."

Those in the family knew he was not being honest. They knew how much he wanted it. To try the rationalization of denial to cover what he may have felt was a failure in selling his own home only set up confusing currents in his wife and children. The man was trying to fight the loneliness of not having attained what he expected. One has to sympathize with him in that. But denial of the dream as having ever been there is no cure for those inner feelings of disappointment. If the family, including himself, had all had a good cry over it, it would have been a far healthier situation.

Self-pity, resentment, rationalization, denial—all these are used to compensate for the loneliness of not having attained some goal. They are all poor tools or even weapons to use in trying to win over, or recover from, the shock of loss in whatever form it may have come.

But then how does one cope with this devastating experience of loneliness that comes with unrealized expectation?

Again, there is a spiritual framework in which these experiences do fall. Biblical characters experienced the same frustrations and reacted as humanly as people do today. There is hope in that, and there can be the cure if the Christian will honestly seek to apply it.

For instance, Paul, the great missionary evangelist, may have waked up one day at the peak of his career to find that he was going blind. There is no specific statement concerning his reaction to that in human terms. But if anyone had the right to *expect* something from God other than that, Paul did. No one was more faithful, loyal, and sacrificial in proclaiming the gospel than he. No one had suffered more than he in carrying out the commission given to him of God. One can only imagine Paul's human questioning: "How does one go on a missionary journey blind?"

Paul's reaction to it was human for 2 Corinthians 12:8 says, "For this thing I besought the Lord thrice, that it might depart from me." Paul was not frantic about it, but he made his appeal to God—and it may well have been a desperate prayer time for Paul too—that God would not allow this to come on him and frustrate his expectations of continuing service. Blindness, of all physical maladies, is a shocking plunge into loneliness. So much of the world is cut off, lost forever. So much of a man's work is dissolved. The same is true of any illness that debilitates and immobilizes. It brings isolation from a big part of life. Cancer frightens the victim and pushes him rudely off the center stage of life to agonizing hours of helplessness. Heart attacks strike quickly and leave the individual weak, disoriented, often bedridden, and simply "out of it." To all of this the individual is prone to cry out, "Lord, why me?"

Paul did not. He may have cried, even as a man, as he sensed his vision going. He may have spent hours in prayer asking for healing. He may have suffered moments of acute loneliness in the realization that he wasn't going to be able to keep going very long on this commission that had given him so much joy.

But Paul did not spend time in self-pity or resentment. There is no indication of that. He prayed and made his case before God. It was not a failure on his part that accounted for it. He perhaps sensed his expectations were not going to be met, so he adjusted the best he could. At that point the Lord answered him, not in granting his request, but in giving him the promise: "My grace is sufficient for thee: for my strength is made perfect in weakness" (2 Corinthians 12:9). With that assurance—that whatever his expectations of healing, they were apparently nothing compared with such a promise from God—Paul added, "Most gladly therefore will I rather glory in my infirmities, that the power of Christ may rest upon me" (2 Corinthians 12:9).

It sounds all too simple for the devastation of disappointment that strikes hard at the person hoping to reach that one goal of fulfillment in life. But *acceptance* of that disappointment in terms of the attitude that says God can make up for it in some other way, is critical to recovery.

That man who saw his "dream house" fade away should have said, "Well, maybe the Lord has something else in mind for us." That is not denial. That is acceptance of the fact that what was so eagerly looked to is perhaps after all not the best. That is not rationalization. It is a statement of confidence that even if there is disappointment, God can and will heal that in time and provide something perhaps far better.

If Paul had wallowed in self-pity or even denial, his missionary career would have undoubtedly ended right there. It was in his own realization that "all things work together for good to them that love God" (Romans 8:28) that he avoided crippling emotional shock in being deprived of expected health to carry out God's commission.

Claire's first reaction to the fact that writing a novel was not for her (at least right now) was refusal to accept it, and denial. In so doing, she also refused to accept the fact that she had other gifts that would compensate for not attaining that dream. After all, only God knows whether that novel would have been a success or failure. Suppose God was sparing Claire the demolishment of having a novel published that did not sell at all. There is hardly anything more painful. Even more painful than not being published is to be published and not be read. In fact, it was this point of awareness that brought Claire back, finally, from her four months of resignation to death. The truth of this point dawned upon her, that God may have indeed refused her own human level of expectation in order to spare her a more intense experience of pain.

It did not come easily for her, but as she put it, "I suddenly realized I was shrinking into an invalid in my refusal to accept the fact that I would not attain the goal I had worked toward so long. In a real sense, what I was doing was denying God the opportunity to bring something into my life that was beyond my own human expectation. I had to grab on to that, or I would die in my self-pity and my 'poor me' attitude. It took all the courage I never really had to climb out of that bed and face life again. But when I did, I found God right there—I'm back teaching, and somehow it seems right. I write educational materials, and there seems to be a keener sense of satisfaction in it. I now and then still dream about that novel—but if it is going to come for me, I will let God guide me to it again. It is enough that I am finding new horizons, and that He is filling the void in my life with meaningful and creative activity."

And what of the minister who, after losing out on his "dream church" went into six months of withdrawal, then into resentment, and finally reprisal?

"I left my calling," he said, "and sold furniture for six months. I figured if God wasn't going to look out for me, I'd look out for myself. No more big dreams about big churches.

And no more scraping the bottom of the barrel in those little churches. I'd make my living my way. It was childish. I was more miserable selling furniture than ministering to fifty people in a country church. I was lonely, empty, feeling that I was on a meaningless track. I was mean to my family in my misery. Then one night when I was flipping through my Bible for want of something to do, but more because drawn again to the wonder of its power, I came across the complaint of the laborers in Matthew 20:12. They questioned as to how the owner could pay the same amount of money to those who worked from the early hours of the day that he did to those who started late. Their expectations were not realized either. They had a right to expect more for working longer.

"Yet the owner said, 'Friend, I do thee no wrong: didst not thou agree with me for a penny? Take that thine is, and go thy way: I will give unto this last, even as unto thee. Is it not lawful for me to do what I will with mine own? Is thine eye evil, because I am good? So the last shall be first, and the first last: for many be called, but few chosen'" (Matthew 20: 13-16).

Jesus does His own no wrong, even in the unrealized expectations. That minister was struck anew by that truth. As he continued, "At that point it seemed that the elements of human expectation were far short of what God has for His own anyway. I still found that hard to swallow. But at that point I felt He was not deliberately doing me wrong, that I was surely wronging Him. Maybe a big church would have given me a big head anyway—but that was denial or rationalization. No, I told the Lord right then how much I counted on that church, but if it was not for me, then He would surely come back to me with those things far beyond all of it. So six weeks later I quit the furniture business and went back to a little church of 125 people. Far from the dream, but still we are happy there, and I have never ministered among people who are so warm and eager for the Word."

Consider, then, the many saints of God who have missed out on a golden dream, then put it before God in the hour of tears and frustration and found themselves possessing something far more precious that the other perhaps could ever have given them!

As Walker put it:

> Half of our blundering futility and self-pity comes from our unwillingness to stop and to think. . . . We react to situations without thinking or praying; we do not respond creatively to trouble in what the Gospels call "the power of the spirit." There is a glorious word from a wise man that was written for our condition: "For still the vision awaits its time . . . if it seems slow, wait for it; it will surely come, it will not delay" (Habbakuk 2:3).[2]

God is mindful of the human frailties of His own in the hour of disappointment, when they cannot rise above it, when there are tears and the loneliness that comes with loss. He does not judge the child of God who goes through the vexing times of disappointment that sometimes gets close to bitterness. But He seeks to communicate the great fact that the loneliness and frustration need not be forever. If the Christian is willing to wait before Him, trust Him, lay the tears and frustrations on Him—and then take from Him that "sufficiency"—the sense of being disconnected, that feeling of "separation anxiety," can be replaced.

Even John the Baptist suffered his moment of confusion and disappointment in having his expectations unrealized. Considering that he was the forerunner for Christ, one could say he should have known better. But the human frame is the same, and that is what the Bible teaches. After John had charged Herod with taking Herodias to be his wife (Luke 3:19), Herod threw John into jail. It was not what John expected. His anticipation apparently was that, as a great prophet sent of God to proclaim the Messiah and preach repentance to all men, he would know complete deliverance himself and judgment on Herod.

So frustrated was he in finding himself in a prison cell instead that he yielded to the human factor. He asked his disciples to go to Jesus and ask him: "Art thou he that should come? or look we for another?" (Luke 7:19).

John was so shattered by this experience that he actually began to question a truth he had proclaimed earlier, that Jesus was in fact the Son of God. When the disciples came to Jesus and told Him what John wanted to know, it did not disturb Him. He knew what John was going through in his hour of disappointment—especially since John knew Jesus, as the Messiah, could pull the jailhouse down in one puff of power, if He so willed it.

Jesus' answer was pointed and significant: "Go your way, and tell John what things ye have seen and heard; how that the blind see, the lame walk, the lepers are cleansed, the deaf hear, the dead are raised, to the poor the gospel is preached. And blessed is he, whosoever shall not be offended in me" (Luke 7:22-23).

In other words, Jesus did not run to John to try to counsel him and get him to straighten out spiritually. Jesus knew that John had to have this hour by himself, to "sort it out" alone. There is a time when a person must make his own journey to find truth. As for John's sense of expectation of deliverance, Jesus sent word to him that the only real expectation for him or any other Christian is to do the will of God.

If one is to die for an act of courage in the faith, then so be it. Jesus Himself would shortly face Gethsemane and know His own terrible moment of facing death. He knew it had to come. Yet when confronted in His humanity with the specter of the cross, He sweat blood, as it were, in the contemplation of it. Humanly speaking, He found it difficult to look to that kind of expectation, the grimness of it.

What could John really expect? What should he expect? Something besides prison and then death? But what was that, considering what he had been allowed to do for God as His forerunner? Jesus said to him that all anyone in God could expect was to minister healing, to preach and prophesy. To be bailed out of jail by Jesus, to be relieved of every pain and disappointment, is not in that list for the Christian. Such expectations are beneath the divine plan for the children of God. There is something far better.

Whether or not John understood the message, the Scriptures do not say. But one has to believe that somehow it got through to him. The expectations he sought from Jesus were purely human, and there was something far greater, part of which he had accomplished already, and much more would be his as he passed through death to eternal life.

Jim Carns came down with bone cancer at the age of thirty-two. A dynamic youth worker who had accounted for the winning of many to Christ and, more, the helping of thousands of young people to find their way, he took the news "like a jolt to the solar plexis." He remembers the tears, then the denial, then the resentment.

"I went the whole route," he said. "Then after my fifth time into the hospital, and when it looked as if it would be my last, that I would never get out, my crying to God to heal me just stopped. I suddenly became aware of all the people in this cancer ward who had nothing or no one to hang on to. Children and adults, young men like me, all lay in their loneliness of pain and coming death. Somehow, right then, I figured I'd better grow up, that there was something God had for me to do there. I quit crying for a break from God and started moving among others to help them realize that Someone did care for them, that death was not so bad to face in Him—it took a while to get up and do that, when when I did, I never ever again prayed for God to heal me. I had found my place for the time I had—I was touching broken people, giving them hope in the Lord, helping them face the glory of death in Him."

When Jim Carns was almost in a coma, he smiled up at his father, standing by his bed, and said, "The last four months, Dad, have been something—really something. I wouldn't have missed it for the world. It's not exactly what I had in mind a year ago—but God had something here for me far beyond what I ever had when I was walking around full of life. I helped a little boy with leukemia laugh today—it was his first laugh in a year. It has just been great to be able to help people laugh with God at death—just great, Dad."

When Jim Carns died that day, nurses cried openly on all the floors of that hospital. Many would never be the same again—for the touch of life that Jim Carns left to them in Christ was something far too precious to ever forget or let go. He had given to them great spiritual expectations beyond their own limited human levels.

For the Christian, expectations will always remain on the human level until God is allowed to reveal His own. There is no progress or fulfillment in those who allow disappointment in the frustrated human dreams to say, "Expect nothing, and you will not be disappointed." Rather, in those hours when

dreams dissolve, when the gold at the end of the rainbow
turns to lead, when the loneliness of disappointment moves
in like a cloud—it is at that point the Christian rises with the
psalmist and says with full assurance, "My soul, wait thou
only upon God; for my expectation is from him" (Psalm 62:
5).

That Vietnam POW has found new healing in his "waiting"
on God and today has fought his way out of the bag of loneliness and bitterness into a new dimension of understanding
with the psalmist. Jane is not yet out of her struggle of disappointment. She is not yet fully confident that she can fall
in love or be loved or married without her ability to bear
children. But as she put it, "I am alive—God saved me from
something worse in surgery. I will never know why I had the
problem in the first place, but that does not concern me as
much anymore. I figure I am no more worthy to be spared
than others. But maybe now my attitude is changing; I love
my work more; I sleep better. I can pray now with an open
heart—I will wait and see what He wants me to do."

Loneliness need not last forever—even in the frustration of
unrealized expectations. He has something in mind, something beyond the human mind to comprehend. What seems
a total loss for the moment must be seen as Paul saw it when
he said, "For our light affliction, which is but for a moment,
worketh for us a far more exceeding and eternal weight of
glory; while we look not at the things which are seen, but at
the things which are not seen: for the things which are seen
are temporal; but the things which are not seen are eternal"
(2 Corinthians 4:17-18).

If this is the attitude of God's own toward disappointment,
then, as Clark Moustakas put it:

A dying spirit must be mourned, a broken pattern of life must be healed, the living embers of one's self must be ignited again. Then the poem that is born will come from a heart and spirit and mind that anticipates a new life, a beginning: and the words of this poem will bring a unique message if we can but hear it and let it enter in its pure form, just as it is, and move us to our own response.[3]

FIVE

The Loneliness of Faith

He had been on the road five months. He still had three weeks to go. Behind him were weeks of meetings and night after night of weariness that would not be assuaged by fitful sleep. There were long days of preaching, visiting orphanages, the slums, the ghettos of Asian cities seemingly caught forever in their misery. Cities like Calcutta, Bombay, Djakarta, Bangkok, Manila were all a blurred montage in his mind—of unrecognizable faces, of people reaching out their hands to him for a touch of life, or for bread, or just to feel someone who cared. By the time he reached Hong Kong, he was haggard, pale, and down twenty pounds.

Why was he doing it? Why should *he* feel the constraint to respond to the needs of these masses of Asian people, Christian and non-Christian, who pleaded for help? Why should *he* preach and evangelize among a people not his own? Why could not one of their own culture and nationality do it? "Because no one of their own has assumed it yet," he said. "Until someone does, one of us has to—if we don't, then who? Do we wait? How long? Does God wait for everything to come together just right?"

One could tell he had been over these heavy questions too many times already. He was from South Carolina. He had a wife and three daughters there—waiting. What about them? He does not answer quickly on this; no quick scriptural rationale now, no hasty spiritualization. He thinks a long time,

86

just staring at the floor. The deeper shadows of loneliness cross his face then; they have been on his mind too. Finally, "They're with me; they stand with me," but there is just a trace of uncertainty as he says it, and maybe he is wondering if he is doing right by them. Five months away from them this year, three away next.

Of course, he is but one example of the many who know the experience of acute loneliness in the faith. Some, perhaps, take upon themselves the exotic business of world travel where others could minister better, even those in other cultures. Perhaps it is true that some men, in the name of God and the faith, thrive on jet lag and find that traveling is their "life call." And yet, for this South Carolina man—"It's what God gave me to do. If I could, I'd exchange it all to be home right now. But until someone else comes along, sent of God, to do this, I have to remain faithful."

The loneliness of faith is the kind of "separation anxiety" that is often the most difficult to bear. For some it appears to be a contradictory term, because it is presumed that anyone who responds to such a calling can never really be lonely. Is not God all-sufficient?

Yes, God does prove to be all-in-all, but at the same time the human frame, "going it alone" against the tide, is subject to intense pressures in terms of that human dimension. Sometimes the man of faith feels his aloneness when those of the church, perhaps, charge him falsely with neglecting his family. Sometimes the uncertainty of whether the "calling is really sure" can plague the mind and heart. Sometimes the sense of whether anyone really cares (that someone is putting family, houses, and lands behind to carry the cause of Christ) can bring a sense of aloneness.

"Sometimes," the South Carolina man admitted, "I wonder

why I shouldn't be trying to provide a more comfortable way
of life for my wife and children—even for myself. I wonder
sometimes if I am doing right by them. In my lonely times I
start thinking whether in the end all that I am doing is really
accomplishing anything. These may be all simply the result
of the pressures I am under, because on other days God
speaks peace to me. But humanly speaking I feel I am in the
desert a lot in my soul, in my mind, in my whole view of what
I am doing here. That may be wrong, but I don't think so.
It is part of the price, I feel, of commitment."

And what about the wife of that man, who remains in South
Carolina, who has the responsibility of shepherding children
and making decisions for them, for the home, even for the
future? While her husband is circuit-riding the churches of
Asia as his calling, she must negotiate an equally difficult time
of being father and mother to those entrusted to her.

"To tell you the truth, I never thought it would be this
way," she admitted. "When he felt the burden of God to respond to the work of taking on the broken, neglected lives of
the world, I thought it would be a time of continual blessing
and bliss. I had visions of sharing in a great harvest of people
being touched by God through him. And I believe there is
that harvest, but having to face the nitty-gritty of the palpable matters of the now, I cannot see all of that. I have to
trust God that it is happening, that's all But since he committed himself five years ago to this work, I have been alone
most of the time. There have been the practical, sometimes
pressuring matters of bills to pay, illnesses with the children,
some frightening, and critical decisions to make. When he is
home a couple of months, maybe three at the most, we hardly
get to know each other before he is off again.

"You ask if it is worth it?" she adds with a faint smile, the tired lines showing around her eyes and mouth. "Well—a life of faith has to be worth it in the end. I hang on to the conviction that it is right. Of course, there are times I pray for more togetherness in the family, for more normalcy for the children in their growing years. I pray that my husband will be home more. I didn't count the cost of all this in the beginning—but I've added it up since, and though it almost seems too much to bear, yet as long as the burden of God remains on him, it must remain on me. I accept it and trust God to keep us going."

Just two people out of the fabric of lives "going it on faith"— one sagging wearily on his bed in Hong Kong, thousands of miles from his family; the other sitting quietly in the modest living room at home, trying to evaluate the long hours of separation. They are objects of either pity or admiration. To the world they are insane, for the world has long since lost interest in sacrifice to such an extent. To the church on most days they represent glorious commitment and vindication of the church's mission. On other days, however, some might call the sacrifice a bit "impractical" and something "certainly not exacted by God." But for them, as "tough" as it is, as painful as it is, to be "all out for God" in these human pressures, it is not so simple to conclude their sense of mission categorically right or wrong (or impractical), wise or foolish. They simply press on with the light they have, asking only that those who care for what they are doing at all will remember them in the hours of loneliness. To them it is not a question of simply turning back from the calling because of perhaps mere human longings and needs. Some do, of course, and no one can judge them for it. But others push on, believing that it is for them to do so.

For those who give themselves to a life of faith, of living

wholly for God, of committing themselves to the task of evangelism or missions, the cost is seldom added up in terms of loneliness. Shortage of cash, the inability to enjoy material things, the possibility of not providing proper educational opportunities for the children—these are the things that most feel will have to be faced. But to feel alone in the task, or as one missionary put it, "to realize that there are no times of applause from anyone, no fitting into the social whirls of the good life at home, never really being a part of people in the normal concourses of life, because a missionary is, after all, a breed apart—this is the crushing load of the cross to me, what Jesus surely must have felt many times, what everybody must feel who puts the hand to the plow. No one thinks of these things at the time of calling or commitment, because we feel it is something God will take care of Himself, and He does— in the end, He does. But these pressures can still bring those moments, those days, of loneliness, and in those times you feel fragile as a human being and even as a servant of God."

For instance, Carl H. left Sears Roebuck after eighteen years of being a successful accounts administrator to head up a small Christian organization. For Carl H., at forty-six years of age, it was the culmination of years of prayer and careful consideration of the Scriptures. In the nine years of being director of that small group, which seeks to provide educational materials for the national church overseas, the financial track record has been precarious. In the last two years of his administration, Carl has seen the financial balance sink to almost zero.

"I would sit at breakfast meetings with other directors of organizations like mine," he recalled, "and hear them talk about their million-dollar grants or how they finished twenty or thirty thousand dollars in the black. I listened to them talk about success and how God was blessing them, which was in terms of money, and it was then that I felt alone, terribly alone. I was glad for them, of course. But I never dared share with them that I was barely keeping my head above water, because that would only have indicated there was something wrong with my faith. Why was I getting pennies while they got thousands? I kept asking. What was wrong with my organization, seeking to help poor nationals overseas? Was it not of God? If not, then what was I doing in it?"

That was one part of the loneliness of the faith that Carl experienced. But he added, "An even more difficult part for both my wife and me was when the friends we once had at Sears were no longer coming around. Even those who had admired us in the early days for responding to the call of God to a mission work began to pull back.

"Yet," Carl explained, "when the people you used to go to Florida with every winter realized that you wore the same suit year in and year out, drove the same old model car, and kept the same furniture, that looked as if it were to collapse any minute, you can kind of expect them to figure we were no longer candidates for the good life in Florida. They were right, of course, but it still hurts. All my wife and I had left then were those few people who were in mission organizations like ours. We thank God for them. But it's difficult to be together with people who are fighting the same wars every day. Sooner or later you begin to bemoan the problems and start talking about things we'd all like to have and can't. We become the lonely trying to heal other lonely people with the wrong remedies. We did our best, but what we needed desperately were those who were in a different strata who would call us friends and accept us for what we were, people who were simply trying to do a job for God."

Or consider missionary Hazel R., who said, "The worst part of it all is that in twenty years of mission service I never could get close enough to anyone at home to really call him a friend. People would pray for me, as they said, as my name came up on the church's prayer calendar, but they could not pray for me as someone they *really knew*. I never confessed an honest human weakness to anyone, on deputation. Nobody wanted to listen to that. It was embarrassing to them. A life of faith has no human frailties, so everyone assumes. To admit them was to destroy their ideal image of God dominating human chemistry. So they kept me above all that; they would not allow me to come down to where they were. I had to be up on some level in order to maintain their trust in me as their missionary. Deputation then is often a time of tears for me; it always has been. I desperately wanted people to accept me into their inner circles as a person, not a superhuman frontier warrior. I wanted to cry with them, laugh with them. I wanted them to do the same with me. Instead, we met, we talked, we passed each other—I did my act, they applauded, and that was that."

The testing dimensions of a life of faith, in other words, are seldom recognized or, if so, seldom really accepted by the church. The church has come to view it as a "higher calling," and therefore something that is ethereal. It is a mountaintop where the faithful have their private conversations with God and therefore need no other, on the human level. A life of faith means unusual power by those committed, unusual strength, unusual heavenly experiences, gigantic answers to prayer; it is Joshua taking Jericho, David pulling down Goliath, Paul roaring through Asia like Patton leading his tank divisions up the Rhine.

People who "go by faith" are often pushed out of the mainstream of human concourse by their own calling. They are set aside for "higher things," which means they can never really enter the valley again to the normal human exchange. Their act of dedication to move out under the compulsion of God ironically separates them from the concerns of those who in effect "send" them. Yet no soldier has ever gone to war without the assurance that there is a time to come home; a time to return to friends, to family, to those who love him, to those who wait and eagerly anticipate touching him again and sharing all the grim and the glorious days of conflict.

Of course, this does not negate those at home who do build close ties with the "sent ones," or the "called ones." There are always those wonderful exceptions.

But a man or woman who moves out in faith, nevertheless, must face the crosscurrents of isolation, sometimes even alienation. And the point is that even within the heart of the "group" one can feel shut out, left out, ignored. And it is not always due to an overwhelming sense of awe of those who dare to live by faith, though that sometimes may be the case.

"I feel the conversation going around me, over my head, delivered to other beings here and not to me," confessed one young man who had committed himself to evangelism among youth, rather than taking a lucrative job in the city. "I am to them a strange breed at best; I have forsaken the nine-to-five job to give my time to helping people come to know Christ. That's great, but what organization am I with? I am not supposed to be doing it alone—it's just not done. My wife and family inwardly resent me for doing it, because there is no security for them in this. My friends find my commitment akin to dereliction, an irresponsible act designed to feed my ego. What ego? I gave that to God along with any guarantee of a weekly paycheck. No man who lives by faith, even just for bread to put on the table, has much of an ego very long! So I have become weird to them—to the people here in this social time, even to my wife and children. My small victories for God are not much vindication of my calling to them. I am then a fool, possessed with living an impractical life. I have chosen to go it alone, they say, because I am a loner, a man who does not wish to earn his bread as other men, but to live off the public and the church.

"So now I stand alone in this room, and people and conversation go around me politely, for I am really not one of them, and they are trying to tell me that. That I deal with broken lives, that I try to heal for Christ, that I put my life on the line in dealing with drug addicts and homosexuals, all in the name of Christ, seems to be irrelevant. The fact to be faced for them is that I am forsaking my family to do that—yet we do not starve, we are clothed, we have shelter.

"But I am not *organized*; I am not in a proper *pattern*. I can only be a missionary as I am with a mission, they are trying to tell me. I must become *legitimate*! What does that mean? I ask you, what does that mean? A weekly paycheck from an organization? Would that do it? Does it all come down to that? If I am to be known by them in true friendship and fellowship, if I am to be accepted and approved by them, I have to go that way. My heart hurts as I leave, because I need them; for my spirit is low, and I need strength from them as God-given. Will someone tell me I am doing something worth doing in the name of God? But no one does. And I go on each day alone—silence. From my family, my peers—and sometimes it is hard not to just sit down and cry."

As Moustakas put it:

> It is the terror of loneliness
> not loneliness itself

> but loneliness anxiety,
> the fear of being left alone,
> of being left out,
> that represents a dominant crisis
> in the struggle to become a person.[1]

The loneliness of faith comes with the realization that there really can be no one else, except God, who will enter into the journey. Yes, people are there, people's faces cross the line of vision, some smile and talk politely, try to communicate interest and concern. Some do try, and some do get through. But most seem to remain a long step removed. Sympathetic, yes! But one walking by faith does not need sympathy; it is love, interest, a need for protection, even validation. The one so far out on his own needs to hear, "I am with you! You cannot go so far in your journey that I will not be there in my thoughts and prayers for you! I will lift you when you are down, cry and laugh with you, and share with you of what I have when you are without provision and your heart is ready to break! I will listen to your admissions of doubt, your secret longings, your visions, and I will reach out to you and give healing for the pain!"

And yet, far too often, the politenesses and even admirations without involvement go on, and the man or woman of faith draws no fresh water from those wells. He then must continue his journey or, as some do, turn back. And then those same people will say, "How could he do such a thing as that?"

Martin J. left it all to write. Consumed by a growing concern to produce books that would penetrate society with the message of Christ, he quit his job and took up his typewriter. It was not a hasty decision. It took four years of fighting both job and the writing burden before he finally committed himself. His friends told him that he'd never make it, that "there is very little money writing books anyway, and Christians don't read that much. And nobody has successfully written anything to non-Christians about God or Christ." In a sense, they were absolutely right.

Martin felt constrained to do it. Two years later he had three books out and maybe thirty magazine articles. But the books had not sold well. "You are not exactly writing for non-Christians, and you have not enough spirituality in these books to interest Christians," he was told by his publisher.

"I am trying to write to non-Christians about God and Christ," he argued.

"Too much Christianity in it for non-Christians," came the verdict.

So, at fifty-two years of age, Martin, a very good writer, after five years of writing realized he was desperately alone. Alone in his writing. Alone in his conviction. His wife would say, "Get a job, Martin, like normal people!" His books still have not sold well. Everyone knows it. His Christian friends never mention his writing—they know he has not written anything to catch attention. So the subject never comes up. Marton needs someone to ask him about his writing, even if it is embarrassing to answer. For nobody to ask at all is but to reinforce his failure. His wife finally took a job to "at least put food on the table regularly." That hurts. So now he must stand at the line. He has committed himself to something he was convinced was his to do, but the crushing loneliness of failure has taken root. Lack of support or interest from his own peers has left him beaten, drained, depressed. To go on means only more of the same. To go back merely makes a mockery of God.

One can focus on any number of individuals who every day find themselves as "solitary persons," trying to do a job for

God. An example is the secretary who hardly makes enough on the job with a Christian group to meet her necessities, but who believes it's where she must be in God's program for her. Sometimes all she needs is for someone to realize she is there, a valuable member of the "team" and not just someone who came with the rent. There is the worker who faithfully performs in the "back room" area of the company, who is seldom recognized for anything except when he is absent. There is the one who sticks it out in a life of faith even when demotions come, when faithfulness is often rewarded with a movement downward rather than upward; the pastor who labors week by week, sometimes for a pittance with "no benefits," who is often cruelly criticized, maligned, falsely accused, and finally driven out in shame that he dared to wear a pair of alligator shoes. "Where did he get the money?" (When in fact a shoe manufacturer gave them to him, but nobody asked.)

So then sometimes the loneliness of the journey in faith can lead to that moment of decision—to go on or to go back. How does one deal with the loneliness of not knowing what is right in such a question? Which loyalty does one cleave to in the end? The loyalty to family members and their "right" to the much more stable way of life that a steady income provides? The loyalty to friends who are desperately needed in the long journey, without whom life is empty, almost meaningless, but who at the same time create pressure, certainly by default if not intent, to take on a "normal way of life"? Can a man or woman go on with God even if there is no one who understands, when there is no way to build a meaningful "connection" to those in the Body? Can he go on when the evidence points to the continual negative balances both in the checkbook and in terms of visible accomplishment for God?

Naturally it all depends on the man or the woman who

must face that decision. It is not dependent on other opinions. To go on or go back is each individual's decision in the end, and such a decision has to be made apart from the crowd and the pressures.

There is the man who has worked twenty-two years in a secular office, trying to make his Christianity count for something with his non-Christian peers. In all of those years his honesty, integrity, and sense of fair play based on God's values have not won him many friends. In the advertising business all such virtues are relative. But if he assumes his loneliness in that company is a sign that God is not pleased with what he is doing in trying to live an exemplary Christian life and decides it is easier to abandon the values and "fit in" (or at least abandon the crusade to make them count for something), he may feel less strain on one level but a nagging conviction on the other. Yet, he alone must determine if he is to yield in order to attain some measure of companionship, rapport, and security, or else to accept loneliness and alienation because of his Christian values—and maybe some day lose his job, who knows?—recognizing the cost of his commitment and drawing on the spiritual resources in God. Who is to judge him in the end? It is he alone who must determine before God which course he is to take.

In his case, however, he chose to stay with his values. "After twenty-years of taking coffee breaks alone and eating my lunch by myself—except on those days when we have company business together—do I now decide that it is too much?" he asks. "Supposing whatever seeds I have planted in my feeble attempt here are about to spring forth from this rocky ground into fruit for God, and supposing my decision to compromise now chokes that off—what have I then accomplished in twenty-two years here? Can I not go on a few more for what I believe? And there are some things I can look at under the surface that prove God has been at work here through me—I've kept the accounts intact with honest advertising; the doorman knows Christ because I've been here; somehow God has been allowed to put His footprints on this corporation, and He did it because He put me here for that purpose."

Thomas Dooley, who founded MEDICO and who gave his life as a medical doctor in the jungles of Laos to heal broken lives, wrote to a young doctor this way:

> The world is made up of persons. Internationalism is only a conglomeration of individuals. All individuals yearn for something human. This flings a special challenge to you as there is no more intimate person-to-person relationship than that of a doctor and his patient. Bring the talents of your degree, and the spirituality of your heart to distant valleys like mine. And take back with you a rich, rich reward. Dedicate some of your life to others. Your dedication will not be a sacrifice. It will be an exhilarating experience because it is an intense effort applied toward a meaningful end.[2]

Tom Dooley died of cancer at the age of thirty. But he could still pass on to those coming behind him that a life of faith brings rewards, even in the midst of loneliness and deprivation, when the human dimensions are stripped away. All Southeast Asia remembers Tom Dooley for that sacrifice, and there is today a monument to him in the city of Bangkok. He gained more in love and favor with Asians as an American doctor than all the diplomats, politicians, and military strategists who crossed that land in twenty-five years.

It is incumbent upon every man or woman in the faith who feels the breaking point from the pressures of that solitary walk with God to see beyond the human measurements to that which is spiritually emerging.

Paul himself wrote to Timothy, "I have fought a good fight, I have finished my course, I have kept the faith" (2 Timothy 4:7). And considering the loneliness of this "fight," one cannot argue the point. And he adds, "Henceforth there is laid up for me a crown of righteousness, which the Lord, the righteous judge, shall give me at that day: and not to me only, but unto all them also that love his appearing" (2 Timothy 4:8).

But put that against his days of frustration and loneliness. He goes on to remind Timothy that he must keep his calling in that perspective, that he must endure the crushing sense of human deprivation if he is to know that glorious eternal value.

"Demas hath forsaken me," Paul says in verse 10. Then, "Only Luke is with me" (verse 11). *Thank God for the one!* God always seeks to provide at least *one person* who will be there. The Christian in a life of faith who is hooked on the "crowd mentality," the "admiring populace," the "back-slapping pals," even "the royal entourage" as endorsement has not caught the sweep of servantship. That "one" is the precious seal of God on a lonely man's or woman's life of faith, be it wife or husband, child, peer, even someone like the custodian, the least of them all, who takes the time to say, "I appreciate what you said—what you did—just for staying in there when everyone says to go home."

But here is where the Christian Body needs to function. Some in the faith are not even sure they have "one" to stand with them. The presumption that all who accept the life of faith are surrounded by a host of well-wishers and admirers is a dangerous one; the human side of such committed people is fragile, and it can break easily. If the decision to go in faith is to be positive, then that one standing at the line needs someone at the critical point to be a truly faithful friend.

Someone should be by the side of that wife in South Carolina, strengthening her in prayer, encouraging her in the long days and nights and the times of doubt about making wrong decisions during the absence of her husband.

That husband of hers, exhausted and lonely in a hotel room in Hong Kong, needs someone to help him lift his feeble hands, which droop even more in his loneliness and perplexity as to whether he is doing right for God when it costs so much in his family.

The writer who lost his sense of purpose, who has not one to keep the fires burning within him, needs someone who will tell him, "Keep the vision alive; we are with you!"

That mission director who feels smaller and smaller against the big organizations that crow about monetary success needs someone to say, "You are not alone, friend and brother. We know and appreciate what you are doing, and it is great! Keep the faith!"

Does not a businessman who has stuck by his Christian values in a hostile secular business for twenty-two years deserve someone who will say, "I know it must be a lonely road you are on. But I want to share it with you. I will pray for you every day; and I hope we can talk some time about what you are learning and seeing through your faith in that place."

For that man who has given his life to a Christian organization, and despite demotions that he can't understand, decides that his commitment is more important than climbing the executive ladder, does he not need a word like, "I sense it must be difficult for you at this time in your life. But I want you to know that your dedication in spite of it helps me to be more committed too. In your dying to self, I rise to new life. I thank God for you, and I want to share your road if you will let me."

That young father who feels pushed aside by his family and

friends for giving himself to reaching youth, with no organization or group behind him, needs someone to say to him, "Someday it might be my child you work with and heal—then I will thank God you were there and ready to minister that healing. Now I thank him that you are willing to put aside what you know you could get in the world to give life to someone else. I want to be a part of your life and your work, and I want others to be as well."

Does it take so much after all to be that "one," that "Luke," who is willing to stand by someone in his loneliness? No, it does not. And God continually searches within the Body for that one who will minister in this way. But is there sensitivity to the need? That is the question.

Paul had other problems too. He adds, "Alexander the coppersmith did me much evil" (2 Timothy 4:14). Who has not felt the loneliness of betrayal by someone "inside"? But did Paul *quit* over it? No, he goes on to say, "At my first answer no man stood with me, but all men forsook me: I pray God that it may not be laid to their charge. *Notwithstanding* [or, So what?] the Lord stood with me, and strengthened me; that by me the preaching might be fully known, and that all the Gentiles might hear" (2 Timothy 4:16-17, author's emphasis).

Loneliness and the rewards of faith are all there in those few passages. To endure one is to gain the other. The pattern of life for God's own who dare to push out in conviction to give all for Him is always the same. But the decision to go on or go back is not dependent on human reinforcement altogether. Paul confessed his disappointments and griefs, but he put them aside in the conviction that his cause for God was worth it all. Every person in the faith has to make his decision on that basis, and that alone.

Jim Elliott, who died a martyr's death as a young man at the hands of the Aucas in Ecuador, summed it up very much the same way when he said:

> Sometimes I say to myself,
> I am a believer for nothing.
> But in the hour when I say, I'm quitting,
> Jesus says to me again
> "Believe me, little son.
> Please follow me.
> To my Father's house
> I wish to lead you, little son,
> To a beautiful country"

If loneliness is too much for a man (or woman) who has committed himself to a life of faith, and when there may not even be that "one," that faithful "Luke" at hand, let him consider Jesus, who took the temptation alone in the wilderness. It was a brutal, soul-shaking conflict. By all appearances it "comes off" as just a conversation with the devil in a mountain retreat. No, it was a barren, rocky, empty place, stripped of all vestiges of life. It was no place to face the enemy alone; the desert or craggy mountain never is. Yet He made His choice in that lonely hour to stand His ground. God's will carried cosmic consequences in that struggle. To walk away from it under the pressure of no crowds, no applause, no spectators, no one to stand by who cared, would have plunged the world into hopeless darkness. Redemption would have fled forever from humanity's clawing grasp.

"So in our aloneness," Walker says, "making value judgments and choices we have our clearest commerce with God. Every decision we make touching the lives of others involves God because God cares for persons. Every choice we make between deception and integrity involves God because God is truth, the whole truth. However much we try, we cannot escape God."³

No, that lonely one pushing on in the dark, seeking to hold some of the light of God for others to see, needs once more to embrace the reality of God "being in the midst of." When the reverse tides tend to send one reeling in the undertow, at that point he needs the prayer that Jim Elliot breathed, from Nathan Brown of Burma:

> And shall I pray Thee change Thy will, my Father,
> Until it be according unto mine?
> But no, Lord, no; that never shall be, rather
> I pray Thee, bend my human will with Thine.
>
> I pray Thee hush the hurrying, eager longing,
> I pray Thee, soothe the pangs of keen desire,
> See in my quiet places wishes thronging—
> Forbid them, Lord, purge though it be with fire.
>
> And work in me to will and do Thy pleasure,
> Let all within me, peaceful, reconciled,
> Tarry content my Wellbeloved's leisure
> At last, at last, even as a weanéd child.

"Waiting on Him for whom it is no vain thing to wait," Jim Elliot concluded.⁴ Could that not be the banner over all who walk alone in the faith? See Jesus standing before Pilate, the final transaction of His journey of commitment. There is no one to stand with Him. His disciples have fled. He stands alone before a hostile crowd, a vacillating judge, and the world's concept of justice. His final march to redemption would put Him into the extremity of loneliness until He would cry out in His hour, "My God, my God, why hast thou forsaken me?"

The life of faith is seldom measured in those dimensions.

The mentality has now taken root that all men of faith are heading for heroism of some form or another that in turn will reap great adulation of those within and without the church. The shock of standing alone in some lonely outpost of the world, in some desert area of a secular office, or in activities that tax mind and body to the limit, is not communicated strongly enough in a church gone considerably "soft" on the qualifications for discipleship.

"The will of God," Jim Elliot stated, "is always a bigger thing than we bargained for."[5]

Again, Jesus took the judgment of mankind on Himself alone, knowing it was the will of God. The ending for Him was not defeat but the victory of resurrection. He accepted the terrible loneliness of the cross in light of the redemption it would bring. The cross always comes before resurrection, and it is the same for every Christian who takes that journey, as God determines it, in faith.

Taking all the human props away then (if that be the case), the man or woman living a life of faith, trusting the light he or she has for the journey commissioned by God, is still never alone. That has become too familiar, of course, but the truth still does not wear out with the using. The mystery of the presence of God in such a life has kept thousands of Christians in the bleakest, darkest, most solitary situations on earth. That is why prison cells do not bend them; the heat and sun of the jungles and deserts do not crack them; wind, fire, and cold do not subdue them; the endless, empty prairies or the crowded metropolises of indifferent masses have not deterred them; in it all, the man or woman of God knows the "presence" and the "still, small voice."

It is to this that Psalm 18 refers: "I called upon the LORD . . . He heard my voice. . . . He made darkness His hiding place.

... He delivered me. ... For Thou dost light my lamp ... my God illumines my darkness (vv. 6, 11, 17, 28, NASB).*

The loneliness of faith need not be forever here on this earth. In the midst of bleak landscape and "inscape" of service. He rises to enter in. He brings the conversation and the gladness of the heart of God. To sit with Him but a moment is to know the banishment of sorrow, the retreat of silence, the routing of depression, the flight of emptiness.

Sit a while then, weary traveler on that road of faith! And let Him speak.

*New American Standard Bible.

SIX

The Loneliness of Work

After thirty-six years on the job, Henry H. is retiring.
"Henry who?" For most of the three hundred employees,
Henry H. is a shadow figure. They recognize him only as the
man in work clothes with a huge ring of keys on his belt.
Henry H. has been the custodian for thirty-six years. For
many in the company, the word is "janitor." People do not
know janitors in an organization as they do vice-presidents,
chiefs of accounts, or payroll officers. Mostly they come to
know those who are on their own peer level or those who are
as they are in the "productive elite" of the work force.

But Henry H. nevertheless has his big day after thirty-six
years of nonrecognition by those around him. There is the
usual formality of proper observance—the cake, the coffee, the
decorated table. And there is the gift, the sterling silver
platter with the inscription "Thank you for 36 years of in-
valuable service." Henry is still in his work clothes, because
he has never come to work in anything else in all those years.
He is embarrassed now, not because of his clothes, but because most of the people in the room have never really come
to know what he has done that is so valuable as to deserve the
inscription.

Of course, they recognize him (but they don't really know
him) as the man who fixed faulty radiators or air conditioners.
They recognize him as the man who unplugged drains and
toilets and carried out many other menial tasks that went with

107

the physical plant. He has walked among them, but he was never really known for any significant contribution to the "larger picture" of production and business (so he says). Now Henry H. will move out from them—and few will notice. Some other man in the same kind of work clothes will take his ring of keys and man the broom closet, as it were.

Henry H. mused on it all later, saying, "Whenever there was something to do with heat or fresh air or lights, it was always, 'Henry, take care of this'—or, 'Henry, can you fix it?' I did it; it was my job. Some times I was there long after they went home, painting, making sure they had a comfortable place to work in. None of them ever knew that or probably ever cared anyway. They took it all as a part of their fringe benefits, I guess.

"But being custodian was all I knew. I did it well. But I guess if I had to sum up these thirty-six years I'd have to say it has been kind of a lonely road. Sometimes I wished I could sit down with some of them for coffee—but then, who would want to sit with a janitor, right? Well, I've seen people come and go in this place. But I stayed with it. That's got to mean something in the end, right?"

Of course, it does mean *something* in the end. But the other "something" that Henry needed in those years did not come across. So he will pick up his few belongings, the few well-worn tools of his trade, and slip out the back way, using the same door he has for thirty-six years.

Henry H. probably feels worse because this is a Christian organization, where he figured no one could be taken for granted. But it can happen there too. In a company of more than three hundred employees, with a constant turnover, there isn't time to dwell on any one person for very long. None of those who had been there took time to realize that Henry felt lonely, so they did not feel constrained to make any specific attempt to give him greater acceptance. The larger the organization, whether or not Christian, the more difficult it is to maintain personal contacts in terms of encouragement or even recognition in work performance. This is not to excuse the people there in any sense, but to establish the perspective that can often contribute to a loss of fellowship.

At any rate, it is often said, and rightly so, that the "organization man" (or woman) is often the loneliest person in the crowd in America today. Those at the top suffer the loneliness of decision-making and the constant need to command. Command means necessary detachment from the people being led—as tradition has it—and so the top men find themselves removed, unable fully to enter into any genuine friendships on the peer level and position level within the company, lest there be a mistaken notion of collusion among certain top executives. And certainly there can be no cultivated friendships among those beneath them, lest they be charged with favoritism. As they see it, whatever friendships they find must be outside, with people who pose no conflict of interest. So then for many top positions, the conflict becomes a real pressure point that can and does bring acute loneliness. (See chapter 7 on leadership.)

For those at the bottom of the hierarchy, loneliness stems from the boredom of menial tasks and the failure to attain recognition. For them it is a life of sameness, of repeated motions in far too familiar task roles. For them the question is, Is this all there is for me? Beyond that comes the bigger question, Doesn't anyone really care?

Take the case of Betty R., who, because of physical handicap, sits at one job all day long. Each day she types names and addresses for mailing labels. She never types anything else. Every day it's another familiar pile of names, addresses, and zip codes. Because she is listed as "handicapped" on her employment card, she will not be moved to other kinds of work that are more demanding. She may be capable of more, as she feels, but management has not yet decided on it. Her ailment is in her legs, she insists, not her head. She is grateful for working, but in five years she has come to the place, at forty-one years of age, where she questions her self-worth. As she put it, "There are days when I simply cannot bear the loneliness of the job, the feeling that my life is forever chained to that label-casting machine. The thing is, I don't blame anyone for it. It's just that a person wants to feel there is something else, something to strive for, something higher, even something more creative. The longer I stay on this job, the more depressed I get—and then I wonder what God has in mind, and I guess that's not a good sign, to be questioning Him."

The worst part for Betty R. is that her handicap elicits too much pity on the part of others. To them she is "crippled," so they stumble over each other to relieve her of the stresses of the job. They get her lunch or coffee. But Betty R. feels a sense of inferiority because of the way well-meaning people dote over her.

For Betty R. there is coming a time of depression and withdrawal that could complicate her life even further. In their book *Conquering Loneliness*, Jean Rosenbaum, M. D., and Veryl Rosenbaum explain it this way:

> The despairing person feels totally helpless and hopeless in the face of his certain fate, that of being lonely all his (or her) life. The despairing person bends under this pervasive threat and says, "No one will *ever* care for me" . . . if these feelings of desperation are allowed to run unchecked, they

can become the psychiatric illness called depression . . . depression is real withdrawal from life.[1]

Loneliness that leads to depression leads to destruction of spirit. Even those who hang on to their faith in God can be dwarfed by the sheer magnitude of the hopelessness of the routine job cycle that never changes from one day to the next. Unless her horizon changes, unless her mind and emotions can rise above the press of the limitations her physical capabilities and the job impose on her, Betty R. will ultimately lose her bearings on life.

The Christian organization perhaps has more difficulty than the secular organization in preventing workers from slipping into feelings of helplessness and despair that bring loneliness. On the one hand, the Christian business organization is supposed to be, by the nature of its inception, dedicated to a more personal level of involvement with employees. But as the organization expands, and minds must turn to the complicated business of maintaining a corporation, its leadership is less and less able to pay attention to people. In some cases, it simply is not willing. The product must now become the priority issue while the means to produce it is really expendable, that is, the people. So then the organization loses its ministerial concerns as such for employees and concentrates more on work performances. Products, then, in short, replace people as the top item on the daily agenda.

This priority of product, in the name of God—and one has to sympathize with those who get caught in it—can have more devastating results on those in the work force than would be the case in comparable secular situations. For instance, Edward R., after twenty-six years as product development director for a Christian advertising firm, was passed over for chief director's job. Instead, the company leaders chose a younger, less experienced man to assume the job. For Edward R., it came as a total shock. For twenty-six years he had worked to bring the company to an expansion in sales that gave it top billing among all such companies in the field. He had done that by long, killing hours in the office and at home. He had sacrificed his family life, vacation life, leisure time for "the company." He had done it "unto God as well as for the product." Now to be told he was not to receive what he had worked so long to achieve left him dazed. Now the traffic flow went around him—now decisions were made by others. He had, in his words, been reduced to an "errand boy"; for him, the dream of arriving at the top position was shattered. The challenge for him was over. In the next year, his motivation dropped, his disposition changed, he became withdrawn, and chronic illnesses began to plague him.

In all these experiences there was a devastating feeling of being disconnected from self-worth. In these cases, loneliness came from a sense of failure and rejection. God seemed to be punishing them, because the problem was spawned by Christian leadership decision. Here again is that "separation anxiety," a feeling that what one has worked to achieve has gone. The failure to receive proper reward and recognition for hard work and faithfulness to the task can come down hard on the person's feeling of value. In all these cases loneliness came with the conclusion *"Nobody really cares for me after all."*

But it is not only in organized labor that loneliness comes down like a pall. One writer, for instance, confessed, "I've worked eighteen years at my typewriter—I got more rejections from publishers than acceptances. But when I did get published, it was as if nobody really cared anyway. I had hoped that a writer having scored with a published book would have some recognition for it, that there would be a greater sense of awareness on the part of others for such an achievement that really few get in life. Three published books later, it was the same. It was as if people who knew me were saying, 'So you published a few books—so what?' Writers write to be read and appreciated for the effort—but I found out that all those hours working alone did not really prove the point. I had not gained much at all in the things that mattered."

Or what about the housewives who move through the numbing chores of the day, the endless round of washing dishes, making beds, cleaning house, caring for children? Much of this is routine, unconscious kind of work, that which has to be done even when the person would much rather be involved in something more fulfilling, more challenging, certainly more creative. The feminist movement probably received its greatest impetus from housewives who sensed their own encroaching pall of loneliness in this round of domestic chores.

So then tension and hostility in homes where wives are at odds with their domestic roles, as well as with their husbands who are feeling trapped in organizational roles that are static, finally break out in marital fractures. For these people, work must be challenging, it must be recognized, it must achieve something for the individual beyond a paycheck. Otherwise it becomes a bore, a frustration, and with it comes loneliness.

But granted that every individual must have some of this in work to remain motivated, that status-conferring rewards are necessary now and then, is this pursuit really the critical point in preventing loneliness in work?

Many would blame organizational leadership or church leadership for this problem. Those who control the destinies of people in job roles are naturally the ones to look to for answers. In many instances, this is true. But the tendency to blame Christian leadership or the church traditions for a fractured sense of self-worth in the job leads to bitterness that eventually affects that person's relationship with God.

There is need for those who do command the work forces in various situations to take heed concerning the way people are handled within the business. There is need for the church not to impose traditional views of wives as being solely *domestics* in fulfilling the scriptural law of wives being obedient. There is need for a greater sensitivity on the part of all to the achievements of others within the Body and a willingness to encourage those caught in the boring cycle of humdrum tasks to see their worth in performing those tasks.

However, much of the loneliness a person feels in a work situation, regardless of what it may be, is not unique to that person. Thousands every day perform the humdrum, struggle with routine, remain in the shadows of organizational "nonrecognition." People face their gloomy deserts of unfulfilling task performances every day and plod on regardless.

Walker says,

> We forget that every achievement is nine-tenths drudgery and struggle, and burdens that seem too heavy are more normal than otherwise. . . . Winston Churchill spent most of his life plodding. Nobody thought he was a genius, not by any stretch of the imagination. He rated as a hack writer or second-rate politician, and those around him often conspired to make his intellectual and political journeyings as unpleasant as possible.[2]

The apostle Paul is looked upon through the glamour-view of the bored, "mere functional" people as one who had high adventure and knew fulfillment on the grandest scale. But his recounting of his missionary journeys is hardly a paean of praise for his "job description." If anyone should have felt lonely—and there were days when he certainly did—or even depressed and in despair through the work he carried out for God, he should have.

In 2 Corinthians 11:25-28, 30, he said:

> Three times I was beaten with rods. Once I was stoned. Three times I was shipwrecked. Once I was in the open sea all night and the whole next day. I have traveled many weary miles and have been often in great danger from flooded rivers, and from robbers, and from my own people, the Jews, as well as from the hands of the Gentiles. I have faced grave dangers from mobs in the cities and from death in the deserts and in the stormy seas and from men who claim to be brothers in Christ but are not. I have lived with weariness and pain and sleepless nights. Often I have been hungry and thirsty and have gone without food; often I have shivered with cold, without enough clothing to keep me warm. Then, besides all this, I have the constant worry of how the churches are getting along . . . but if I must brag, I would rather brag about the things that show how weak I am (TLB).*

Paul's life may not have been routine, but it was not at the same time a bed of roses. He had more cause to be in despair concerning his service than anyone in a comfortable office in the safe, affluent, contemporary world that the Christian oc-cupies today.

That does not mean the problem of loneliness in work is not a fact. One businessman confessed, "There are days I would gladly exchange the routine of my work for a missionary's in the wildest head-hunting tribe in the world." It is true that there is more restiveness in a culture that is geared to achieve for rewards of affluence, position, power, or command. Amer-ican society, rapidly moving man ahead technologically has

*The Living Bible, Kenneth N. Taylor.

all the ingredients needed to give people a feeling of dead stop. The Christian feels it more intensely than most, because within him burns the flame of honest desire to serve with all energy and gifts to enlarge the Kingdom of God. Typing mailing labels or being a janitor or changing diapers every few hours may not provide all the totality of fulfillment expected, and there is no argument with that.

However, Walker says, "I dare say most of us spend more time in struggle than we ever are likely to spend in triumph. Life is mostly one routine job after the other. Orloe Choguill comments pertinently that the most dismal thing about milking cows is that the cows never stay milked."[3] That could be said about dishes, beds, mailing labels, and so forth. The businessman never gets to the bottom of the paperwork that piles up every day on his desk. The salesman never runs out of calls, many of which are fruitless. Every day is an endless cycle of the same elements of work that do not change much for any variety or excitement. Such is life.

But how is it then some people manage to cope with all this and not slip into crippling loneliness and depression? How could Paul talk about the "joy" of his work when he was constantly in danger and fulfilling a commission that had all the seeds of depression in the human sense? The answer really comes down to the attitude of the individual and not "*they* who are responsible for this." One's attitude can either be resentment, which breeds more loneliness and depression, or it can be as Paul stated in Philippians 4:11: "I have learned in whatsoever state I am, therewith to be content."

The term is "content," not gloriously, deliriously happy or running over with fulfillment. It is the attitude of acceptance of what is, not in final ho-hum resignation, but in the sense of recognition that this is only a part of the growth process God has in mind.

One key to all this is referred to by Dr. David Reisman in his book *The Lonely Crowd* as the difference between· one who is "inner directed" in his work and one who is "other directed."

"The *inner-directed* person," he says, "is not only chained to the endless demands of the production sphere, he must also spend his entire life in the internal production of his own character ... the inner-directed man is job-minded."[4] In other words, the individual who looks at his or her work only as a job to gain something of recognition in the production elite of that company is "inner directed." The focus is on the job— period.

"The frontiers of the *other-directed* man is people," Reisman continues. "He is people-minded. Hence both work and pleasure are felt as activities involving people."[5]

In all the cases cited earlier, loneliness in the job came about because the individuals were more inner-directed than other-directed. Henry H. constantly referred to his *job*, what he *did*, and the refusal of others in the company to know him as a significant *contributor* to the company. What Henry H. sought was some kind of badge that said he was important in what he performed day by day. If Henry H. had taken on an other-directed attitude, he would have seen his work as a relationship with people, an involvement with individuals, and not simply a performance record he had to fulfill faithfully day after day. Other-directed people, who enjoy their work because it allows them to be a part of others, seldom, if ever, experience crippling loneliness or that feeling of being alienated or shut out. As an other-directed person, Henry H. could have sat down for a coffee break with anyone in the company, because people respond to people—they do not respond to company cogs who are too conscious of what they do versus who they are.

The same could be said of Betty R., who made the label-casting machine her albatross. She was too inner-directed in terms of a hyperconsciousness of her handicap, which became directly related to her inability to advance in the job hierarchy. People who wanted to be kind were put down in her mind as only intensifying her handicap and thus complicating her desires to be recognized for greater abilities. If she had become other-directed, she would have made the rather boring label-casting job only a means to building rewarding relationships with those around her. Loneliness comes when people refuse people, in whatever area of work they are in. *Job concentration* versus *people concentration* and awareness is what frustrates too many people in the work force.

Again, that man Edward R. in the Christian business, who after twenty-six years lost out in his bid for directorship, suffered the same malady. Fortunately, what kept him from serious depression was an awareness about himself and his situation; since he had only thirteen years to retirement, he could either go on sulking over the "bad deal" he had received in his desire to "make the top," or he could turn it around for something good. He decided then to become other-directed, to make his remaining years count for something in other people's lives. His first move was to cultivate the young man who had received the directorship over him and to offer whatever his twenty-six years of experience had taught him. The young man was already feeling lonely in the hostility he had received from others—as well as from Edward R.—because he got the job with such inexperience. He was overwhelmed by the offer. The relationship between Edward R. and that young man became a close one in the years ahead. For Edward R., shifting from "inner directed," a consciousness of the job scale, to "other directed," toward people and their needs, saved him from hopeless loneliness and ultimate loss.

Housewives who dwell constantly on the "dirty job" they have at home will continue to sink in the morass of their loneliness as long as they insist on keeping that focus. The housewives who view their tasks as other-directed see the routines as important to children and husband; what they are doing brings order in the home, and that keeps people happy and together. Housewives who are other-directed in their tasks not only keep a good household but also manage to find fulfilling relationships outside the home that are people-oriented as well.

The writer who lamented his lonely road in terms of no recognition for his achievement was making his writing a means to climb up the community social calendar perhaps. His inner-directed motivations then landed him in the slough of despond. But if he had seen his writing as a means and a ministry to help thousands become better people, his other-directed view of his work would have changed the landscape and "inscape" of his life.

That is why Paul, for all his perilous journeyings, was other-directed in all of them. He said, "Yea, and if I be offered upon the sacrifice and service of *your* faith, I joy, and rejoice with you all" (Philippians 2:17, author's emphasis).

An inner-directed Paul would have said, "Having sweat for you in the ministry, I at least expect a longer vacation with pay and some advancement in the apostolic line."

Loneliness then comes down to the attitude of the individual toward the work, the job, the task. The job is seen either as the whole landscape in terms of reward, recognition, or fulfillment; or else it is seen mainly as a means to be involved with people. There is a vast difference, and that difference determines whether or not a person will suffer crippling loneliness and depression.

Finally, loneliness in work comes about too often by an attitude of self-pity. It is difficult, of course, if a person is inner-directed, not to feel "down" on himself or herself when the job does not "pay off" in terms of advancement and recognition. To break the back of loneliness in the job, one must literally refuse to become morose over the failure to achieve or to climb up the job ladder. As difficult as it is to take rejection by leadership or to fail to get a promotion, it is at this point that the individual must learn to accept what is beyond his control and see it as a part of his emergence as a complete human being.

"The problem of life, therefore, is to handle upsets when and where they come without floundering into self-pity," Walker says.

> The dictionary suggests by way of synonyms that to be upset is to be "overturned, disordered, capsized," or simply to be "mentally disturbed." There is a difference, however, between being "capsized" by self-pity and being "mentally disturbed." It is one thing to be sunk, and it is something else to be troubled. The problem is to work our way through troubles and difficulties without being capsized or sunk. The Apostle Paul expressed the idea admirably when he wrote, concerning the early Christians, "We are afflicted in every way, but not crushed; perplexed, but not driven to despair" (2 Corinthians 4:8)*[6]

No, work, even in the Kingdom, need not breed loneliness

*Revised Standard Version.

to the point of immobility of mind or spirit. Work, for the Christian, is an opportunity to be with people—people are the best antidote for loneliness on any front. People are God's provision for the vineyard—if the individual will see the treasure to be had in that dimension, work can be, even in its most menial dimension, a means to perpetual reward.

SEVEN

The Loneliness of Leadership

Mountain climbers say it often: "The higher up you go, the lonelier it gets." The same experience applies to leaders who, in their climb to the top, have found that the oxygen gets thin, the available companionship increasingly sparse. The plains and mountains and valleys of human intercourse where a man or woman must maintain some vestige of the general can provide territory for acute isolation and loneliness.

If the worker feels estranged and shut out in the mundane, routine tasks of the job, the leader experiences something even more acute—the loneliness of command. The feeling of being alone in the "oval office" with the ever-present demand of decision-making that can affect a large number of people, or the course of a nation, corporation, or even a church, is something acute. It wears heavy on those who either choose to lead or have leadership thrust upon them. For most in such positions there is the feeling of being a "breed set apart," not allowed the luxury of close companionship or fulfillment for some solid connection with human understanding and sympathy.

Richard R. quit the pastorate after eighteen years of service and returned to the business world. Broken in health and feeling he was only a shadow of his former self, he explained, "I realized those years had made me look and feel ten years older than I was. I had spent them holding people's hands, smoothing out countless interpersonal battles and church struggles, preaching how many hundreds of sermons, baptizing people, marrying them, burying them—as the church grew, so did the traffic to my office. I was not surprised at this, nor was I unaware of my calling, the demands I had to face in serving. But in all that time I could not find a confidant, not even my wife—because most of the human problems I dealt with were confidential—or someone who could simply listen and pray with me. While I struggled to find new and fresh sermon material, time for my own relaxed devotional life disappeared. When the church reached 1,200 members from the first 300, it was a sign of great blessing from God on my work. I accepted that and thanked God for it. But at the same time I found myself even more lonely as the demands on my time tripled. My family was growing up and away from me. When I saw my children graduate from high school and then college, and I realized I hardly knew them, I knew then I had to do something, though I was a little late. I concluded I could not abide the lonely road any longer—as much as I sensed I was leaving an arena with its joys and triumphs, as well as its sorrows and tensions, I knew I had to find some area of work where I could establish normal human relationships. Maybe I was just not cut out to be a leader, after all."

Many a pastor has found this to be an all-too-familiar experience. "If there is a solid example of being lost in a crowd, the minister probably fits it best," one pastor confessed.

Paul Tournier, commenting on the loneliness of pastors, stated,

> I have rarely felt the modern man's isolation more grippingly than in a certain pastor. Carried away in the activism rampant in the church, he holds meeting after meeting, always preaching, even in personal conversation, with a program so burdened that he no longer finds time for meditation, never

opening his Bible except to find subjects for his sermons. It
no longer nourishes him personally. One such pastor, after
several talks with me, said abruptly, "I'm always praying as a
pastor, but for a long time now I've never prayed simply as
a man."[1]

Ministers who honestly make the attempt to build rapport
with fellow ministers and hope for some meaningful fellowship find that playing golf with them ends in long theological
discussions or talk of the problems peculiar to each of their
churches. Seldom, if ever, is there ministry, or pastoral care,
toward each other. Sometimes unsure, questioning, and in
doubt, they must nevertheless continue to present that image
of complete control, assurance, and confidence in the pulpit.

"People will tolerate fatigue, mistakes, faulty judgment or
a slip of the tongue in almost any profession but never in the
ministry," one pastor said. "Pastors are looked to as rocks, un-
moved, unmarred by the thousand shocks that rumble around
them every day—they are, in essence, the personification of
God. And that can put a man in a vulnerable and lonely position."

But leadership has its demands regardless of whether it involves pastoring a church or commanding the local Scout
troop. Of course, the loneliness one feels in any single command situation can be more severe than in others. But loneliness is not the peculiar characteristic of one profession over
the other. While pastors must assume the spiritual leadership
of a body of people and minister constantly to a multitude of
needs, the business executive who has command faces other
pressures.

Ronald T. moved up the ladder of a Christian radio station
from production assistant to program director and finally to

manager. In four short years he scaled the heights. Ron was a gregarious man, quick to laugh and joke, wanting to be other-directed rather than inner-directed. With that natural personality he found friends and did much to build the image of the station simply by being a morale builder.

When he became manager, the job changed, and he changed with it. Suddenly he was no longer a part of the "ordinary" work force. He was now directing others, making decisions for them. He was now in an office that was too big, but which he felt he had to fill, and he sat at a desk that was too large and immaculate for his work habits. New people addressed him as "Mister" and not "Ron." The matters of program content and production techniques were no longer his to deal with. He was now working in the "larger picture," concerned with growth and "image" and "listener profiles" and "station philosophy." Now he was signing people's payroll checks, determining budgets, and working with members of the board of directors.

For a man like Ron, who loved people, to be pushed up to the top where people were less important than operational efficiency—so he concluded—the loneliness crept in with disheartening reality. Now he had to play the role of manager, be aloof, maintain protocol, stay discreetly distant from his own executives lest any one of them feel he was favoring one over the other. He took his coffee breaks by himself in his office or arranged to have them with another top executive where the image of the "breed apart" could be maintained. Soon he found himself changing his church and his friends to avoid any personal attachments that might provide a conflict of interest. What new friends he made, however, were much like himself, managers, vice-presidents—conversation with them concentrated on "shop talk," on profits and losses and general business problems that Ron was trying to avoid in his leisure time.

Ron T.'s personality changed with the demands of his new executive role. He was no longer the gregarious, fun-loving, free spirit, ready for a laugh any time. He became somber, withdrawn, quiet, and often crisp in the assigning of work to his staff. He dealt now with people as if they were transistors, pieces of equipment that could be used; when they were not useable, they were replaced. Ron T. in three years as manager shifted drastically from other-directed to inner-directed, and consequently affected his total relationship, even with his wife and children.

Ron became a silent, lonely man, but he would not admit something wrong was happening. Women perhaps are better equipped to share their loneliness on a peer level, but men hide it, pretend it does not exist, avoid any moments when they might become vulnerable. Suzanne Gordon in her book *Lonely in America* quotes Michael Brown, an actor in the San Francisco Bay Area theater group "Moving Men," a group that deals with the difficulties of being a man in America. Brown said,

> A man's whole being is involved in not feeling pain. There's a lot of loneliness and pain inside men that just builds up. It's one ball. It's not disconnected, and if you pull on any part of it all the others start to vibrate because you're touching the whole thing off—touching off everything that has been buried. It's a loneliness ball, because you've got all these things inside you that you won't let anybody see. That's why men avoid things that are depressing . . . because they know if they feel anything negative or depressing it will kick off all these feelings that you have repressed through your whole life.

That's what loneliness is. There is no acceptable way to
feel pain. You have to do it alone, because you can't share
the deepest part of you with anybody. Except maybe with
one woman. That's where you're allowed to express your
feelings. But that objectifies the woman, because she's just
a pillow to cry on.[2]

Concerning the loneliness in corporations, Suzanne Gordon
adds: ["In] the competitive world of business the man must
stay on top of his work, his feelings, and his career. If he has
a problem, there is often no one in whom he can confiue, because to confess to weakness is to risk losing whatever career
gains have been made."[3]

Gordon quotes James Clovis and Pearly Myers of the New
York consulting firm Handy Associates:

We are shocked to see that if you look at the top ranks of
corporations, not only are the women lonely because they
don't have their husbands, but these executive men are absolutely isolated. We know that, because consultants are used
by executives as friends. The entrepreneural types are very,
very lonely. They are in a hostile environment that they are
trying to control, manipulate, and direct. They have good
survival skills because they are extraordinarily discreet. But
they really have nobody to talk to. They don't even talk to
their wives until the day a decision is made to do something
different, like move. They have children who feel they don't
know their fathers . . . so we get very top, successful men
who need someone to talk to. And they also come with personal affairs. That's one of the reasons these services like
financial, tax and estate counseling are so popular, because it
gives the executive a confidant, someone to work his personal
life through with.[4]

But surely none of this is characteristic of Christian corporations. Perhaps not always so acutely, but it is there. As one Christian executive put it, "There is no way to run this organization on the B-Attitudes. The pressure is on me to get performance. If I were to talk about 'blessed are the merciful, pure in heart, poor in spirit,' and so on, somebody would be in here in five minutes looking for a raise in pay. There are people always looking for a way to take advantage of leadership that appears soft. In other words, there is a time and place for the B-Attitudes, but not in an organization like this, even if it is Christian."

When a Christian in a leadership position finds that he cannot apply biblical maxims to his role or in his relationship with his employees, he becomes even more frustrated. (In many instances, of course, leaders refuse to apply them out of an uncertainty coupled with an insecurity in the role.) Finally sensing the futility of it, he surrenders to the "reality of the situation": he must run everything and everyone like a business. This, to him, will help him avoid unnecessary slippage in his command and assure necessary discipline that will produce. Whatever spiritual precepts are to come through will be confined to the morning devotional time, something detached from the business itself, and yet something to validate the organization as being Christian.

In all of this, one has to realize that certain distinctives of leadership cannot be altered so drastically. It is not enough to appeal to leadership within Christian culture to put aside the badges of command and become "one of the boys."

For one thing, leadership, and its attendant qualification of being apart, is necessary to maintain some sense of hierarchical structure without which an organization cannot effectively unite for performance. Any person who takes leadership must assume the cost in terms of the loss of normal interpersonal relationships within that company, troop, church, whatever. Intimacy with those subordinate cannot be indulged in without blurring the lines of command. In short, loneliness is the high price leadership must own up to.

There are too many cases where people who assumed leadership in an organization, be it church, mission, or business, then refused the demands of the role and continued to maintain a far too intimate relationship with employees. In the end, the leader lost his command. While he found reprieve for his loneliness, he also incurred a loss of respect for his position. People no longer looked upon him as one who held their destinies in his hands but only as simply a "nice guy." "Nice guys" can be found in leadership positions, of course, but they can only cultivate that and demonstrate it in the labor relationships inside and in the social relationships outside. Intimacy, in other words, cannot be practiced within the framework of organizational protocol.

Then, again, there is leadership that is set apart by the nature of the position. This cannot be compromised easily, even with the best of intentions. Some leaders, by the power of their skills and unique gifts, inherit a "disconnection" from those around them by the nature of these talents. Position, on the basis of these unique qualities, keeps the leader on a level that does not provide any rites of passage to others below him and sometimes not even on a peer level.

Jesus was a lonely figure in His earthly sojourn because of this. Though He deliberately sought to break through the barriers and open up an intimacy commensurate with His servant role, His own disciples kept Him "set apart" because of His Messianic position. He moved among the people, He loved them, but He, by His role as the Son of God, was regarded with such a holy awe by His followers that He could not gain the intimacy He sought. In the upper room at the Last Supper, Jesus made the greatest single attempt at demonstrating the intimacy redemption was soon to bring when He took a towel and washed His disciples' feet. Yet Peter was aghast and resisted by asking, "Lord, dost thou wash my feet?" (John 13:6). As intimate as the setting was, as beautiful the gesture, Peter could not absorb the enormity of the Messiah acting as servant to him. He did not understand, but he would later, after the cross and resurrection. But at that point Jesus the Man must have experienced some loneliness.

The point is, however, the same resistance can be found among workers toward leaders within Christian culture. The nature of the role of leadership to most of them forbids intimacy. Thus the leader finds himself either pushing the barriers to gain it or withdrawing into the solitary climate of leadership responsibility. The position and the responsibilities prevent the much-needed involvement with others.

There is no denying that a leader, to maintain order and authority, must assume some burden of detachment from those who look to him for command. The role demands it; or the nature of one's gifts and skills presumes it. And, too, the survival of order is often dependent on that careful, circumspect comportment toward people by leadership.

But leadership need not succumb to the inevitable costly loneliness that many have inflicted upon themselves. Personalities do not have to alter to maintain the role. Pressures of command need not drive a leader to throw up his hands and quit because he has been denied the normal human intimacies he is entitled to. Again the Christian work collective operates between two extremes: on the one hand, the leader plays a domineering, "front office" role, ignoring and refusing the needs of the workers and himself in terms of some form of camaraderie; or he insists on being "the nice guy" and creates a dilution of authority so that the business or group soon becomes a law unto itself. While one position brings devastating and unnecessary loneliness, the other offers companionship and hearty fellowship at the expense of the needed strength of command.

Tournier points this out when he says:

> Thus, with relation to the social organization of business, three distinct conceptions face us: (1) the patriarchal or classical authoritative system, wherein the boss gives the orders and the personnel are expected to execute orders received without using their own intelligence; (2) the Communist conception, which weakens the essential order by attempting to give to the personnel the functions of leadership. Unfortunately this is the system so many think of when they talk about re-establishing a human bond between boss and worker; (3) the organic conception, which is as different from the first as from the second, in which there is re-created the spirit of fellowship through face-to-face relationships, without for a moment introducing any confusion as to respective functions and levels of authority. . . .
>
> This third way will restore the dignity and human worth of the worker and strengthen both his professional proficiency and his interest in and attachment to the business as well without the employers having to abdicate their responsibility of direction.[5]

Tournier suggests,

> It is a matter of mutual understanding, of being interested in one another, of each considering the other . . . it is a question of ceasing to fear one another. Because he fears his pupils, the teacher deals severely with them. It is because the foreman fears his workers; that is, he fears being shown to know less than they on a given point—that he cuts off every

discussion with them and finds refuge in silence. He invokes the accepted authority of the boss to terminate an agreement that might embarrass him.[6]

There is no question that pastors are often lonely because there is no face-to-face relationship apart from their own ministerial function. The average church lacks mutual consideration and understanding between church members and the pastor. The people presume a role on the minister in his leadership that forbids too often the minister from entering into their lives apart from Sunday dinners—which frequently put the minister under the gun on some theological issue—or the formal inner-church functions that keep him forever on the fringe. The bigger the church, the less a minister is allowed intimacy with his flock. He assumes the image of a corporation head and not of a shepherd who should look upon them as a flock of sheep needing guidance and succor and fellowship. A shepherd role maintains leadership but also cultivates love and trust.

At the same time, as in the case of Richard R., who finally quit his church because of the crush of loneliness, some need to bend a little toward their own people. Ministers who play volleyball, bob for apples with children, remove their clerical robes now and then to umpire the church league baseball game, do not lose their leadership role, but find it tremendously enhanced. Ministers have an aura of holiness about them that prevents the average parishioner from making the first attempt at intimacy and friendship. *Robert R. played his leadership role at the expense of his human role—he functioned, but he did not fellowship.* The longer he practiced that aloof stance—though he deeply desired more intimacy with his people—the more the people came to accept him on that basis.

While Jesus, by his divine character, maintained leadership, or command, of His disciples, He also told them, "Henceforth I call you not servants; for the servant knoweth not what his lord doeth: but I have called you friends" (John 15:15). While He kept his authority as the Son of God among His own, He declared that His relationship with them was also— or even more strongly—that of intimacy in friendship. This is a classic example of the "organic conception" of an organization characterized by a spirit of fellowship rather than by simply an employer-employee or servant-master relationship. This friendship may have been slow to take hold among the disciples, but it inevitably altered their attitude of holy awe of their Lord to one of true discipleship, which is respect and love working together toward Him as leader and toward each other. Their own loneliness would remain if they were allowed to qualify themselves solely as servants with regard to Him, or mere slaves to the Kingdom. Friendship gave them heart for the work and greater love toward Him.

Christian leaders who fear friendship as being an invitation to disrespect by the workers have lost the spirit of Christ in this regard. Friendship at least allows a leader to call his workers by name, to show interest in their problems and their progress. Some pastors of large churches who refuse this level of relationship with their flocks, because it might invite a dilution of authority, take unto themselves a far more lonely road than the people intend for them. Pastors who see people as faces but not as names, and who maintain that view, do in the end suffer crippling detachment and then exhausting loneliness.

So, too, in the case of Ron T. He allowed his leadership role to result in an alteration of his personality, which in turn brought him loneliness and disconnection from people he once knew intimately. Executives in leadership roles who have sensed the need to balance their authoritative responsibilities with more intimate friendship with the workers have come to view the worker in "mutual understanding and consideration." Friendship for these leaders means inviting workers into social occasions outside the job, such as company picnics or bowling league competition.

Ron swallowed the myth that detachment and isolation from his workers would guarantee fewer problems for himself and less threat to his leadership role. It actually added many more he had not anticipated, within himself, because his "inscape" became more bleak as his outward panorama seemingly became more organized.

One leader of a large Christian manufacturing firm once a week takes time within the workday to walk around his plant and converse with his employees. His questions center on them personally, how they like the work, how things are going at home, or questions to those who might be having problems of illness within the family. This gesture builds friendship out of a concern for them, and it also builds respect for him as a leader because he is willing to share their feelings beyond company work functions. The leader and the worker, on this level, then experience a fulfillment of the need for "mutual consideration and understanding." That is why some workers say, "I would be willing to die for that man."

The refusal or failure of leadership to become more considerate of those under it is summed up by S. I. Hayakawa, who stated, "Perhaps in a very important sense, as D. H. Lawrence charged, we have lost touch with our passional selves; we have lost the ability to know each other at the nonverbal level, looking at each other's eyes, touching each other's hands, and feeling each other's presence and responding to each other—rather than to each other's titles!"[7]

When General Eisenhower committed his crack paratroopers to jump behind the lines in France prior to D-Day, he said to his aide, "I can't let them go without a part of me going with them. Let's go down and talk to them before they take off." Eisenhower did just that and gave to those men, many of whom would die, an intimate touch with the Supreme Commander. The great general became for that moment a field soldier. In that moment Eisenhower was free from the loneliness that hung on him in the top echelon of command as general. Without that touch, without that sensitivity, without that gesture of being one with those under him, the leader may falter under the sheer weight of loneliness. And those under his charge likewise sense their own loneliness in not having this identification.

No one can say categorically when that moment comes when intimacy with those in the line brings a dilution of authority. But leadership that seeks to lead out of understanding and concern for his own need not fear a loss of respect. Of course, there are not always enough times when a leader is completely free of that shroud hanging over him by the nature of his office and the position that must be maintained. But leadership is a responsibility, not simply to the machine, or to functions or performances, but to people.

The leader cannot survive in an authoritarian stance that keeps him or her always apart, detached from the worker. Something inevitably dies in him, something of God and life, the things that matter. Yes, there are times, many times, when the leader must accept his moments of loneliness that go with position and decision. But there are other times, maybe many

more, when he can reach out and touch someone, even one
who is the smallest part of the "kingdom" entrusted to him,
and in the touching know once again the wholeness and completeness of his soul. Christian leadership, perhaps above all
others, must come to terms with this. Clark E. Moustakas put
it this way:

> Sometimes it is necessary
>   For one person to touch another person
>   in his lonely struggle
>   To enable the person to gain
>   the courage and strength to act on his own.[8]

When this happens there is a kind of transformation, as
Tournier notes:

> Again, the man who has passed through the Christian experi-
> ence is freed from the parliamentary spirit. Because he has
> dared to face up to himself, he no longer fears men, nor does
> he fear to discover their true selves behind the social mask
> they must wear. Like Socrates, he tests not their ideas but
> the men themselves. He brings into being thus, with his
> friends and with his foes, an atmosphere of fellowship in
> which agreement, instead of endless disputes, is possible.[9]

Jesus did that time and again. He put that ahead of His
leadership as Messiah. He never worried about losing His
authority in so doing; He never resisted the human touch out
of fear of being used, as a result; He never avoided it in fear
of appearing to be less divine because that touch was all too
human and intimate. It was for this reason He could pray
that prayer of exultation in John 17:11-12: "And now I am no
more in the world, but these are in the world, and I come to
thee. Holy Father, keep through thine own name those whom
thou hast given me, that they may be one, as we are. While

I was with them in the world, I *kept them* in thy name: those that thou gavest me *I have kept*, and none of them is lost, but the son of perdition" (author's emphasis).

This is not the prayer of a lonely Savior. It is a prayer of joy in the knowledge that He, as the divine Leader on earth, has experienced the wonder of drawing men close to Himself. In that earthly journey He took the time to eat with them, drink with them, fish with them, to share their sorrows and their joys, their assurances in Him and their doubts.

Jesus "kept them" in God's name. The leader who can bend to the stature of the Son of God in leadership and humanity will never know crippling loneliness. The man, however, who uses his office to dominate others, to build his own kingdom by using others; who pursues the myth of leadership, even as a Christian; who says he must be removed, detached, withdrawn from those God has entrusted to His charge, is to know nothing but an agonizing emptiness and total aloneness.

Perhaps for the leader who suffers in the long hours of the night, cut off from human attachment, forced to face the load of his leadership alone, Seneca has the best expression of commiseration and the best counsel:

> For who listens to us in all the world
> Whether he be friend or teacher, brother or father or
> Mother, sister or neighbor, son or ruler, or
> Servant? Does he listen, our advocate, or our
> Husbands or wives, those who are dearest to us?
> Do the stars listen, when we turn despairingly
> Away from man, or the great winds, or the seas or
> The mountains? To whom can any man say—Here I
>   Am! Behold me in my nakedness, my wounds, my
> Secret grief, my despair, my betrayal, my pain,
> My tongue which cannot express my sorrow, my

Terror, my abandonment.
Listen to me for a day—an hour! A moment!
   Lonely silence! O God, is there no one to listen?
Is there no one to listen? you ask. Ah, yes,
There is one who listens, who will always listen.
Hasten to him, my friend! He waits on the hill
For you.[10]

For those leaders who have not yet caught the reason for their loneliness, it would be well for them to first climb that hill and find Him who waits to listen. Having been there, no man can return and be the same again; that holy place, that encounter with Him who said, "I call you not servants . . . but . . . friends," can and does provide a whole new panorama of possibility. The hill is not a lonely one anymore; and the landscape and "inscape" of the leader will never be a lonely plain of endless horizon. Instead Christ can open up a world of fulfilling command and friendship at the same time. Such is a big part of the redemption He bought for man.

EIGHT

The Loneliness of Diminishing Time

He woke up to the sense of emptiness. Silence. The house remained in that shroud of mournful vigil. For a long time he lay there propped up on one elbow, listening. He had always listened—for the sound of the baby in the room across the hall, the sound of Tim turning over and bumping the wall, the sound of Jill grinding her teeth over some unpleasant dream.

Now nothing. The house creaked in the wind. That was the only sound. Age. The sound of age. He glanced at the clock. Nearly 5:00 A.M. He was always up at six. But he felt no anticipation of that hour now. What was there to get up to? The baby, Georgie, was gone now to college—Tim was flying for the Navy, already having arrived at manhood—Jill was a nurse in Boston. They were no longer here to get up for. The laughter was gone, the shouting, the giggles. The chirps of excitement that children gave to mornings, that tingled the nerves of parents and said life was full of meaning—it was all gone.

Time had wiped it out. There was only the big empty house and passing images, a life having been spent. Only the ticking of the clock and the gray dawn seeping through the curtains, neither of which held any fresh promises for the coming day, remained.

This was the way he felt now at the grand old age of forty-nine. Like thousands of others, men and women, there had come that sense of near terror of being disconnected from

139

what was and even what is. The sense of separation from the
organic union with children is sometimes almost akin to
death. Children mean life, continuity, a sense of permanency.
They mean that time is still in place, never moving. But when
they are gone, the sudden awareness that life has been clock-
ing the hours relentlessly can and does leave many a parent
suffering a dull ache, a painful sense of loneliness.

For others the experience may come in the middle of the
night, when silence again hangs broodingly, and there is that
sudden awareness, a kind of "mournful reality," that life is
spilling away. There is no inventory to take now. The precious ingredients that kept life a challenge are gone. There is
only the bed and the night and the fearful contemplation of
the end of life. In that moment, again, there is that ache for
all the dreams unfulfilled, all the mountains not yet climbed
and now never to be climbed. In that moment there is a feeling of helplessness in the face of what can never be brought
back, of what cannot be changed.

Sometimes the realization of time having gone and its attendant loneliness can come with even a more devastating
jolt. Richard B., for instance, explained it this way: "Suddenly our first six children were gone, and we were alone,
facing each other for the first time in twenty-eight years. All
our married years were spent trying to talk to each other
around our children or through them. We had become ac-
customed to it, to them, to the demands they made of us.
Their lives were ours. We could not visualize life without
them around the table. And now there we were, just the two
of us, facing each other at breakfast. And it struck us both at
the same time. We were all we had, just the two of us. We
were suddenly so overwhelmed by our sense of loss and loneliness that it took a good ten minutes before we could say

anything to each other. We were conscious acutely now that we had to start over again, only this time our time left had to be spent with and for each other. In that moment both of us felt an uncertain kind of fright. It was not that the two of us couldn't abide each other; it was simply the shattering sense of awareness that time had truly caught up with us."

Still, again, the loneliness of diminishing time comes with the realization that the time of planting and harvest is gone. Some find themselves unable to cope with the fact that they *are* older, that the people they once knew as young are also older. Many have died. A new generation has taken the stage—new styles, new language, new interests. And with that comes a sense of sadness in the realization that there is little room in the world for those who are "older." The young in today's American culture—though not all—have little time for those near fifty or over. The gray head is not a mark of wisdom or distinction; it is a sign of decay, decline, of a breed that no longer has significance in the new order of things. Where other cultures revere their aging parents, in America the gray head represents, too often, the dying bull elephant pushed off from the herd, left to find his own way, to find his place to die alone. And who has not seen that in the nursing homes in this country?

Some, of course, take drastic steps to reverse the inevitability of all this. Some take crash courses in the nuances of the youth culture, hoping thereby to fit back into it. Some cling to their children, almost desperately, either moving closer to them or having them "live in" for a while, "until you get settled." This mounting pressure of being disconnected from life, from purpose, from meaning, that time seemingly dictates—yes, the terror of having to face the awful truth of that diminishing time *alone*—has driven some wives and husbands to breaking points with each other.

Then, with this, comes that creeping sense that what was once familiar ground with familiar faces is no longer there either. Joan Crawford, the actress—a person one would not expect to experience loneliness—in her later years commented on this in an article for *McCalls* (August 1977):

> There are times when I wish someone would ask me to dinner. I wouldn't always go out much anymore, but just the pleasure of being asked would take all the loneliness out of an evening. The older woman, especially a widow or a single like me, is a social liability . . . you can only impose upon your children or close friends so much of the time—the rest of it you have to hack by yourself, and there are only so many books you want to read or TV shows you want to watch or records you want to listen to or memories you want to revive. Sometimes the walls close in on you.

Again she recounted, "Everything in this apartment I shared with Alfred . . . out there all I find is ghosts. Say you're driving through Beverly Hills and you spot a house where close friends lived—you can't stop because those friends are dead or they've moved and some rock star lives there now."

Others, of course, perhaps more men than women, feel the sense of age as a waning of youthful strength and vigor and even interests about life that once kept them sharp and very much alive. There comes with this a fearful consciousness that the body and the mind are wearing out, and with that a sense of growing uselessness to the job and to the community. Some men will try to compensate by frantic efforts at reeducation for new job skills or go all-out for dangerous exercise programs to trim the muscles again; some women will try facial massage to take away the wrinkles and go on crash diets that too often make them ill. Still others give it all up for a life of retreat, of withdrawal, to the television or the study, to a time of mere motion, to existence, rather than life. Some just fade and wait for death. Or some slip into nostalgic moods, trying for recall, playing records of another era over and over again, hoping to recapture some of the wonder and adventure that once was youth.

"I felt only that something had broken," one man of fifty-one years said, recalling the moment of painful awareness that said to him he was no longer going to fulfill his dreams. "It seemed I had always looked forward to the time when my children were grown and on their own, and I could then settle down to what I always wanted to do. But suddenly I realized that though my children were grown and gone, I felt that what I wanted to do was for them, not really for myself. And now at fifty-one, they did not need what I wanted to do for them. They did not consider it important to them. Without a reason to do that thing of my dreams, I suddenly felt cheated; and then I sensed despair, because I couldn't do what I wanted to do anyway. My time had passed. The reason for it had passed, and the time to do it had passed. Suddenly I felt old and useless, and I had no more dreams. I felt I had dropped into a pit with no way out."

These experiences of the sense of diminishing time are as true of Christians as non-Christians. Christians suffer the trauma of seeing their children grow and leave home, just as non-Christians. Christians sense the passing of time and the changing panorama of the environment, the values, the norms, the traditions just as non-Christians. There is often the same experience of fright at what age is coming to mean in unfulfilled dreams, the shock of the empty house, the facing of reality in terms of the breakdown of the body or mind. Emotions, after all, are the same in all men and women; the difference for the Christian is not in experiences but in the *reaction* to them. How a man or woman faces into the wind of these inevitable changes in time is critical, and it is here that the Christian can call up something of immense value.

In any case, the Christian need not apologize if he should sum up his feelings much as Clark Moustakas put it:

> Where are those sounds and movements of love and life now? The halls are deadly silent. Faces no longer appear. An important pattern of living has ended. It is difficult to breathe. I am separated: I am alone. I can feel the loneliness of a living, breathing world that I helped to create and became totally involved in, that no longer exists. Somehow I must let go of that world in which I was once firmly rooted. But how? To be alive, to be human, to create life, to commune with others, to know the depth of dialogue—and then suddenly to face only the dark, cold, quiet emptiness of floors and ceilings.[1]

Ira J. Tanner added to this by saying, "Time also changes the quality of our experiences. It is impossible to recapture or recreate the exact same mood, excitement, or atmosphere of a particular experience now past. In no way can we relive it now as we experienced it then. Oh, we can try, but somehow the quality of that experience will be different. Time dictates that."[2]

It all comes to attitude—how a man or woman faces into the realities of diminishing time. A person's life can be over at any age, depending on how that person views the totality of life's rhythms and patterns. Those who sink into the quagmire of despair over the fact of change both in time and in life can die all too early. Though they may function, go through the motions, inwardly their "inscape" clouds the total landscape of their lives.

Actually no age level signals an end to growth for the Christian as far as God is concerned. Usefulness, purpose, and meaning are forever present even in the shifting tides of time in the life of His own. The degree changes with the phases of life, but depending on how a person draws on the new perspectives of these phases, there is always within reach the wonder of transformation.

When Paul said, "Therefore if any man be in Christ, he is a new creature: old things are passed away; behold, all things are become new" (2 Corinthians 5:17), he meant first of all the experience of regeneration that comes when a person comes to know Christ. But was that all? Is not one aspect of all things becoming new a continual process in other dimensions besides the strictly spiritual? The Christian who has come to know revolutionary change in Christ, from death to life in the spiritual dimension—is he or she not then in a position to catch that "newness" in the totality of life, regardless of age? If one's attitude recognizes that God is renewing with time and not simply allowing regression, there can be continual realization of new dimensions of life never before experienced.

A housewife, confined to her chair because of paralysis in her legs due to an automobile accident, caught some of this in her mid-fifties. Every day she sat on the front porch "looking out on life," as she put it, watching others participate in it while she slowly succumbed to the endless hours of uselessness and boredom.

Then one day she caught something different happening around her. First, she took the attitude that God had a level of experience for her that could be had in no other way than through the position she was now in. She could not see anything different at once. And then, she said, "On this early fall day, I began to watch the leaves on the maple just beyond the screen. Each day they took on new hues, from yellow to light red, to brilliant red, and finally to a rich rust color. Then one by one they gently left the branch, having given the world a show of astonishing brilliance. It was a glorious, even audacious, act of God trying to give witness to those of His own too busy to see that age and changing patterns of life only heighten the splendor of living.

"Those leaves accepted the inevitability of their return to the earth. But in so doing they took on the immensity of God and in those moments knew the wonderful synchrony of Him at work in the universe, even in the smallest forms. All things in harmony, all things in season, all things filling a glorious purpose, yes, even in the denouement of time. For as the leaf left the stage, having given of itself in that brief period of splendorous transformation, it now gave itself to earth, giving life to produce new life."

For that housewife, whose sense of diminishing time was so real in terms of her ailment and her years, it was a moment of revelation into the mystery of God's rich and rewarding cycles for His own. Such experiences are never beyond the grasp of anyone who wishes to probe beneath the surface, who will sense that there is more to life than a sense of time running out and with it an accompanying feeling of decay and drabness.

God's dimension of life is never bound to time, or age, or even physical limitations imposed. That is why Rachel Byron at eighty-one and in a nursing home still paints on canvas every day and produces some of the most breathtaking landscapes. Every day for her is a "new look" at the wonder of God through eyes even more alive to that other "dimension" than in her prime years of creativity. That is why Albert

Schweitzer in his eighties was still composing new anthems to the glory of God on his old reed organ in the jungles of Africa and was still doing it the day he died.

No, there need not be obsession with the emptiness of purpose or of fulfillment—and with it the shriveling up of the human spirit—that the passing of the years seems to dictate.

So, then, to become suddenly aware of an empty house, children grown and gone, to sense a palpable shift in those "tides," to be jolted with the realization that it can never be the same ever again, does not and should not precipitate full stop to any individual, certainly not the Christian. Those empty places that time has now created do inflict painful reminder of loss, of course. It is not wrong to feel that sense of mourning, of loss, of strange sadness and loneliness.

As Ira Tanner put it,

> Dietrich Bonhoeffer, a clergyman who spent several years in a concentration camp in Germany during World War II, wrote in his book *Letters and Papers from Prison* (New York: MacMillan, 1967) that there is nothing that can fill the gap when we are away from those we love and that it would be wrong to try. Speaking out of his own personal experience, he said that even God cannot fill that gap. Irreligious? Some may say so. But no person can ever be *replaced;* it is impossible to find another exact duplicate. If that were possible something would be taken away from the uniqueness of the original relationship.[3]

In other words, God sets in motion all that will occur in one lifetime for any person. Each phase comes and passes, and what is left from that time endures on its own. There will always be the memories and those moments of experiencing the touch of those now moving in their own worlds. But in this span, children are born, grow, and move on. For those who are left, those who bore them, it is now a time to look to the new tide coming in, new events, people, experiences that are designed to provide that unique treasure of the fullness of the years.

God is never finished with His own, then: life is not a reel of film that rolls slowly down to the end, each scene becoming more and more faded until the last is totally dissolved. Consider from the biblical record how God pushed aside the so-called dictates of time and age in dealing with His own. "Now Joshua was old and stricken in years; and the LORD said unto him, Thou art old and stricken in years, and there remaineth yet very much land to be possessed" (Joshua 13:1).

From that point, Joshua—an "old man"—went on to divide the land accordingly. So what was age to God? Nothing. Time is His to give and His to use. It is up to His own, again, to lay hold of that correct attitude that will prove the point: that God does not retire anyone from life any more than He retires from the continual acts of creation He designs in all phases of a person's life. This attitude, then, should be one of growing excitement as there is the realization of potential for new adventure. Many are finding this to be a fact in their own experience. "Retired" craftsmen go on to mission fields to share their skills with national Christians. Others become houseparents at colleges or children's homes. Still others find that the years have prepared them for rewarding work among the ill, the lonely, the poor.

Again, in this regard, consider Abraham, who at seventy-five years of age was settling down in Ur of the Chaldees. A man that age had the right perhaps to fold up his tent and allow the creeping shadows of "useless old age" to dominate him. But God had other ideas. He called him out of Ur to a "land that I will shew thee" (Genesis 12:1). The only "land"

Abraham expected to occupy right then was his rocking chair. In fact, so entrenched was he in this attitude that God had to call him *twice* to get moving. No one knows if Abraham continued to argue the ludicrousness of "trying something new at my age"; but the point is that he finally did obey and entered into the greatest adventure of his life.

It is then a question of facing self in these moments of pressuring loneliness, of realizing that the fears of uselessness and weakness that come with passing time are unfounded and that to imbibe them is to miss the crowning point of life.

The loneliness of diminishing years need not be at all. There will be times, of course, when every person will remember, think back, hold to the joy of former things. These are all part of the treasure of God. There will be times of longing for loved ones far away, times when there is that "sentimental mood," the clinging fruit of a life well spent.

But none of this should bind the human spirit in loss. These moments are given of God, remembrances to fulfill the years, but more than that, they are indulged in only as fresh fuel for moving on to higher ground.

Any man or woman who will allow God to make all the years rich in new experiences with Him can know a companionship and accomplishment that transcends the changing human scene.

Perhaps Morris L. West in his book *The Devil's Advocate* summed up best the reality of diminishing time and something of the attitude to take in facing into it. His character Monsignor Meredith said:

> "Let me tell you something important . . . it is no new thing to be lonely. It comes to all of us sooner or later. Friends die, families die. Lovers and husbands, too. We get old, we get sick. And the last and greatest loneliness is

death, which I am facing now. There are no pills to cure that. No formulas to charm it away. It's a condition of men that we can't escape. If we try to retreat from it, we end in a darker hell. . . . But if we face it, if we remember that there are a million others like us, if we try to reach out to comfort them and not ourselves, we find in the end that we are lonely no longer. We are in a new family, the family of man."[4]

And one could add the family of God, rightfully and truthfully. For that is where He is, and that is where He wants His own to be. To move away from the ash heaps of diminishing time takes the will of mind and spirit. The ash heaps symbolize what has gone, and every person wants to dig around there for bits and pieces of life gone by. But there is no heat in that ash heap. It is now cold. What warmth is left is in the heart of the man or woman who has taken from that dead compost the preciousness of what once was.

Now it is time to let history rest, to guard the values it gave on the one hand but only to make them multiply over again to someone else. The man and woman who find this attitude and move with it come to know a level of human companionship and love, a life filled with people who eagerly reach out for the precious springs of life being offered. The grace and beauty of growing old is tied directly to that attitude. Those who ignore it shrivel up all too quickly and fade away in their separate prisons of defeat and melancholia. Those who lay hold of it come to know the transformation, a certain "newness of life" that provides a new plateau for fulfillment.

This is what God intends. It is His promise that the loneliness of diminishing time need not be at all, and if it is there, it need not be forever.

NINE

The Loneliness of Illness

"It's when the lights went out and the room was suddenly plunged into darkness that the awful awareness came. The traffic of the hospital went on like an uncontrolled fever outside the door, but inside that room it became still, so that you could sense the walls and the room itself growing smaller.

"I was never a lonely person up to then; at least I don't recall being lonely. But now I knew what it was. My family had gone home together, to the familiar, safe place. But I was here alone, isolated from them, facing the uncertainties of what hospitals mean. Up to this moment I had joked and laughed with friends and family, because it all seemed a kind of lark. But now I knew. And I suddenly swallowed hard against that pressure in my chest; I was a little girl again, wanting someone to put on a light somewhere, to cut the darkness, so I could get to sleep. I became terrified by the feeling—and sleep was a long time coming—hours of trying to push my mind off the emptiness, the fear, the darkness, and now the hospital itself slowly growing quieter, almost eerie, until there was only silence."

Perhaps not everyone has that kind of feeling in hospitals or experiences the loneliness of illness to that extent. But sooner or later every individual comes to know some of it, the sudden anxiety of a life being pushed aside, a body unwilling to function in some vital part. The bravest of souls have come to know the shock of the body no longer in harmony. The realization of that has a vast range of effects on the emotions, but most agree that this "separation anxiety," this feeling of being totally disconnected from what is supposed to constitute normalcy, is a jolt.

Sometimes the feeling begins with denial: "This surely can't be happening to me!" The mind says, "This surely cannot last, it's a small thing, they won't have to operate after all, and I'll be going home tomorrow." When denial does not alter the fact of the illness, rage takes over; now it's the mind shouting, "I've never been sick a day in my life! Somebody's made a mistake!" Or else, "If this is all there is to it, forget it!" Others roar, "I've been good all my life, watched myself, kept myself from extremes, exercised, ate well, didn't drink, smoke, or engage in any vices—so is this what I get for it?"

So when denial does not alter the condition, and rage expends useless energy and likewise falls on deaf ears, then comes that pit of despond called self-pity. It is at this point that loneliness and depression are ready to take hold and hang on. This is more dangerous, because now there is not the will to fight, to rise to the battle, to marshal all the forces of courage and optimism necessary to bring final healing.

This all occurs in the emotions, or in the "inscape," of a sick person, because man has come to believe that the body is a machine that goes on and on. Others falter maybe; others need repair; but each individual takes peculiar pride in his or her own chemistry in that it seems invincible, can endure any stress and strain, and will go on forever in perfect synchrony.

It was the Chinese philosopher who said it best: We are endowed with a body that is

> self-nourishing, self-regulating, self-repairing, self-starting, and self-producing, lasting like a good grandfather clock for three-quarters of a century." Further, he says the body is

provided with "wireless vision and wireless hearing. It has a system for filing reports and impressions through a vast complex of nerves. It goes about with perfect knee action, and its amazing motor is completely silent.[1]

So then, when illness comes to disrupt any of that perfect synchrony, God's masterpiece, the individual feels some confusion, uncertainty about the temporal elements within the body, and then a growing doubt that leads inevitably to fear in some form—mostly the fear that whatever is impaired within may take away a part of life forever.

But then again loneliness is not spawned only in the illness itself. Others find that the sudden plunge into the total anonymity of a hospital strikes hardest at a self-contained, self-sufficient individual. Now he or she has been reduced to being just one more body suffering some inner displacement. Now it means being fed by others, washed by others, and probed and stuck by others, hour after hour.

A 280-pound tackle from a professional football team lay in bed with a serious back injury. After two weeks of such an experience, he finally broke down and cried like a child, while being fed by a nurse. "It just hit me," he said, "that I was totally helpless whereas only a short time before I had it all together. I suddenly felt like a baby in a high chair, and something snapped inside, whatever it is that keeps a man believing he's a man. To lose my self-sufficiency broke me."

Or again, as one forty years of age put it, after lying for two-and-one-half weeks in a hospital, recuperating from a serious heart attack, "Everything about me was on a chart. I wasn't a name, except when they had to remind themselves and check my wristband. All of my body chemistry, its mixtures, was on that chart. They knew what my blood was like, what pills I took and when, what my elimination habits were; they even knew through a monitoring system how I breathed, how my heart reacted to every move. All of what was supposed to be me was on a chart bound in a leather jacket. But no one bothered to know me really, that I was a gregarious person, a person who liked to laugh; or ask what made me cry, or if I liked to fish or go boating or go to baseball games, or what kind of food I liked to eat—none of that was relevant. I was not a person but an object for sticking and probing and testing and experimenting. They stood over me and hummed or grunted or sighed or whispered in corners. But seldom did anyone tell me what it was they discussed—it all went on that chart. So I was left to my own imagination of what was wrong, how serious, and whether it meant a life of inactivity, with my job on the line or becoming a burden to my family. After a while I sank deeper into the doldrums. I thought I was strong enough to lick anything that happened to me, but lying there day after day with my fears playing havoc with my mind and emotions, I was actually reduced to being a child. One night I let the tears come, and that was a shock, to realize I had come to a place of such total helplessness and despair and anxiety that I lost control of myself."

Illness and forced confinement in hospitals where nurses and doctors appear to view each body as only a body, can and does cloud the "inscape." This in turn affects the total landscape of the moment. Weakness prevails over what was once strength; the mind is boggled where once it was clear and quick and ready. There comes with this a sense of total vulnerability due to the fact that nobody says when the illness will be better, when it will be time to go home. Sometimes it comes in terms of the loss of self-image, when the body is exposed to the view of all concerned. "Spending your life clothing yourself for the sake of modesty," as one person put it, "trying to find the best fashions to dress it up, all unravels in the mockery of that horrible contraption called a hospital smock."

Again, all of this strikes at pride, the pride of "having it all together" and now realizing it is coming apart. The loss of self-image, the loss of self-identity, all, if allowed to play on the mind, lead to a loss of hope. With this inevitably comes loneliness that destroys the will to push on, to get well, to find some point of optimism in it all.

In fact, when anyone ill allows himself or herself to dwell on this separation from what is normal to life, it can and does increase the problem of healing.

William R. related his experience this way: "I had a growth removed from my neck, which proved malignant. The report struck me hard. Like others, I went through the denial process, that someone had made a mistake; when I knew it wouldn't change the report, I went into rage and took it out on nurses and doctors and even my family. Despite the doctor's assurances that they had gotten it all, that it was not large, that it had not spread, I still felt they had done me in.

"When they finally decided to ignore my tirades, when nurses came to my room only when it was absolutely necessary, when my family found visiting hours tense, I sank into a sulking mood. Now it was a time when I kept repeating to myself, 'Why me?' The more I kept asking it, the more I sank into self-pity. I began to see myself slowly being eaten up with cancer. I thought of the coming pain, the isolation from friends, the long, hard months of waiting to die. I began to withdraw, became unresponsive to nurses, visitors, hardly conversed with my family. I became angry with the attempts to buck me up, with those promises of doctors that I had a better-than-90-percent chance of never having cancer again.

OK, so what about that big 10 percent? Instead, I began to let the curtain of loneliness drop between me and life and people, those around me. I had succumbed to the inevitable—death.

"The days grew longer and the nights darker. I refused to eat. Three weeks later I was told the incision was not healing. It was not a return of the cancer, I was told, but that I was not mustering my body and mind and emotions together to help in the cure. If I wanted to remain in depression, they said, chances were I might have a long time waiting for healing. And as one doctor put it, 'You can complicate the surgery and even grow another cancer, as has happened, if you continue to dwell morbidly on it.' "

Fortunately for this man, the shock of that news got to him. Somehow, as he put it, "I began to climb slowly hand over hand out of the dumps. It took me a long time to shake off the weight of depression I had allowed to come in. But as I struggled to make it, I found nurses and doctors right with me helping me as I made that climb. Now my battle had become theirs, and willingly. Today, eight years later, I am free of cancer, but I am convinced I would not have been had I allowed myself to continue in that attitude of what I called *protective loneliness,* a willful desire to withdraw into a shell in hopes of shutting out the uncertainty and fear that hung on me day and night."

So no one can totally divorce himself or herself from the loneliness of illness. A common cold that put a vigorous person to bed can be the breeding ground for feelings of isolation and loss. The terminal patient, of course, feels it even acutely, and rightly so, for life is in fact slipping away. But every individual needs to be aware that there are going to be times when illness, whatever the degree, will plague the nerves, but the severity of the strain on those nerves and the degree of loneliness that comes are dependent on the ability of the individual to see it all in its perspective.

Otherwise, who is to account for those who do rise above the grim circumstances of illness and find some measure of truce with it? What is one to say about those confined to wheelchairs for life, but whose attitude is a sonnet having a greater sense of lyric and melody than that of those who are walking around in full strength? They have their days of loneliness too, of being cut off from what is normal living, but they are never crippled by it. There are those many, who refuse to succumb to the reality of "being out of it" by the tragedies that strike their bodies, who learn to accept what is, and this gives them a radiating aura that draws others who, even in good health, need the benediction they bestow.

It is this attitude, once cultivated and drawn upon, that does save many from the demolishment of illness. For one thing, these individuals do not consider themselves a mere number on a chart in a hospital. Charts to them are incidental, though significant to those in charge. Charts to them are the necessary part of finding the problem and curing it. These people shred the anonymity of a progress chart by cultivating those around them, by projecting their own selves to them. People remain people, in other words, even to those who must so often work with the blood and other chemistries of those in their charge. But as one patient put it, after facing a leg amputation due to complications of diabetes, "I found that I became something more to those caring for me as I considered them much more than people simply doing a job on an inanimate object."

Those who refuse to make their beds or their wheelchairs or their pain a reason for self-pity are those who have, in many instances, transformed the very people who kept their charts and found their jobs could be a delight because of the attitudes of such patients. These patients in turn have found that their illness then has ultimately drawn concerned care—that nurses and doctors are really pooling all their resources and knowledge to heal a *person*, not a thing.

To grab on to this fact is the first great step in defeating the crippling forces that come with the fear and uncertainty of illness that demands hospital confinement. Sometimes people who have gone through the "toughest" experiences have learned something transforming to their lives, something they would have not known otherwise.

One man who had open heart surgery and went into a critical seventy-two hours following surgery said, "I was not always sure where I was and who was around me, or caring one way or the other which way I went. Yet I found later, at the height of my critical hours fellow Christians all across the community had joined in all-night prayer vigils that I might pull through. I had never known so many people even knew me, let alone would want to take the time to pray for just one more sick person in the hospital. Others, to my amazement, came to the hospital lounge to stand vigil through the long nights, hanging on to God for me.

"In the middle of the fog, when I wasn't sure I was going to make it, one nurse would appear in front of my face, with the most angelic smile, and hold my hand and tell me I'd be all right. I thought if this was heaven, then I'd gladly stay. I found that she and the team of surgeons and cardiac specialists who stood by my bed all night and into the next day were not simply viewing me as another case or a number on a chart. I was to them a person they wanted dearly to see win the fight, and they were throwing all their knowledge and skill into the line to make it possible. Teams of nurses in the intensive care unit later cheered every time I made some new progress.

"The days that followed were days of people's being constantly concerned for me, night and day. I was never out of danger for a good ten days, but they never stopped hanging in there with me, doing everything possible to make sure I'd have it all going for me for complete recovery. I came to love every one of them for every gesture made to give me comfort and restoration. Without that experience, perhaps I would never have known truly how committed professional medical people want to help a person through the loneliness and uncertainty of a critical illness.

"There were times of postoperative 'downs,' but the messages of love and prayer continued to bolster me and give a new sense of my own worth to others. Even that nurse who had stood by me in the critical hours took the time after her hospital day to stop by regularly to check blood pressure and heart. For her it was out of love, and because she knew I needed the assurance that I was coming along well.

"Some say there ought to be an easier way to find out who your friends are, and whether doctors and nurses are more than automatons. Maybe there is. But I would not have come to this 'heart changing' experience without it—and maybe God knows sometimes that is the only way."

When this attitude of confidence in others—that they really care—prevails, there is then what Walker says:

> Nothing, I am sure, is more important in the healing process than the grace of acceptance and relaxed surrender. When we accept the fact that we are dependent on the competence and care of others and on the healing grace of God and stop protesting, a gentle conspiracy of nature, human com-

passion, and God take over for our good. When we give up trying to manage our own cases and relax in trust all the resources of nature and God rally to our defense. We literally commit suicide with protest and tension; we are saved by surrender.[2]

Christians need to be reminded of this attitude as much as anyone else. The man or woman of God is subject to the same battering of fear and accompanying loneliness, except there are those resources available in God that others do not have. However, it is dishonest to claim that every Christian suffers none of the pains and darkness of those outside the faith. Even though the Christian knows that God "doeth all things well," and that Romans 8:28 works all the time, yet the human factor can sometimes overwhelm these assurances. The experience or even the contemplation of *pain* can reduce the strongest of faithful hearts to tearful children. It is a great mistake to refuse to admit to the inner fears and anxieties of an illness, to "play it tough," or to exude great confidence as if God's public relations image were on the line. It is in fact the admission of these fears and uncertainties even in the midst of faith that brings God closest to the individual in need.

One man who had to have a special test to determine if the arteries to his heart were blocked went into the hospital, smiling all the way in the assurance of his faith. In the three days prior to the test, he read his Bible, joked with the nurses, scoffed at the test and what complications could ensue, and simply repeated, "Nothing really worries me about it. I have the Good Shepherd with me all the way." That was true to be sure, but when the man was wheeled into the X-ray department for the arteriogram, he suddenly went to pieces. It took some time for him to get settled down, and one of the attending physicians, a Christian himself, who knew of the man's "boast" in the Lord said to him, "All right, now, Otto, you have finally become human like the rest of us. Remember what the apostle Paul said: 'When I am weak, then am I strong'" (2 Corinthians 12:10).

It was a lesson in the fragility of the human factor that that man learned. Christ does not expect His own to bite the bullet in times of stress, hoping thus to appear to be a proper credit to Him. The confidence of God is a sure strength; but a heart that lays false claims to inner courage instead of honestly admitting fear is denying a needed childlike attitude toward God, that attitude which He is quick to minister to. It does not mean a person falls apart in his faith; it does not mean becoming so apprehensive and fearful that God is denied His power to affect the situation. There is surrender and confidence that He will do what He will do, and that He will do it well, in His time and according to His purpose. But, again, there is no shame in feeling uncertainty or even succumbing at times to pain with a groan that at least indicates that God has not yet made the Christian into some kind of "bionic" man or woman.

This leads to the whole purpose of pain in an individual's life, and the attitude that seems to prevail in those who carry it every day and yet manage to rise above it. There is no mind-over-matter means to overcome pain; there is no self-hypnosis that will change it. And certainly pain is not a signal of evil in the life, nor is it inflicted always as a form of chastisement of God for some sin. He may do that, of course, but pain often accomplishes something in the life that can be done in no other way.

Much has been written on the problem and purpose of pain. But suffice it to state that it should not be viewed as strange for the Christian or something to which faith has created an immunity. It is in suffering that God is often closest. Many a Christian in the throes of desperate pain has known the wonder of that closeness when a cry of, "Please, God, help me!" rings out to Him in the middle of the night. Some do not always know the same sense of relief. But in it there is something occurring, something emerging, something of the mystery of God's own suffering for mankind that is coming through. Pain that is not realized in the context of God's presence is meaningless, empty.

There is powerful truth in what the psalmist wrote: "Before I was afflicted, I went astray: but now have I kept thy word" (Psalm 119:67). Accepting pain as God's corrective measure has given people who needed it a new measure of themselves and a new perspective for life.

Hebrews 5:8 says of Jesus, "Although He was a Son, He learned obedience through what He suffered" (RSV). It would seem strange that the Son of God should have to learn obedience by affliction, but, again, His own human factor was as much a real presence as that which His own sense today. Out of His suffering came a new power, the power to move to the cross and redemption. It is true that some men of the faith never get their commission from God until they see it through hours of pain. It was in Christ's suffering on the cross that salvation was released to the world. Pain, then, is not a waste to the Christian; song writers, authors, poets have done their greatest work out of suffering. They rose with it and above it and released something of creative power that the world came to know as treasure. All great poetry or music or art or praise has at its heart the core of human suffering.

Finally, it is in pain that triumph comes to others. Isaiah wrote, "He was wounded for our transgressions, he was bruised for our iniquities. . . . He was oppressed, and he was afflicted" (Isaiah 53:5, 7). Nevertheless, "with his stripes we are healed" (Isaiah 53:5). The Lord took it all so that mankind would one day know the triumph of being set free from the bondage of sin and self that spawns fear and death every day.

As Walker put it so well, "Somehow the great sufferers have saluted, marched on in lonely grandeur with the mystery of their suffering, and found the 'strength' that is 'made perfect in weakness.' They have had the courage of soldiers and more, and in God's grace they have marched to triumph with their eyes open, fixed upon the hills of God, whence comes their strength."[3]

That is why the author goes on writing even though she has only six months to live, and from her pen come beauty and power that will live for ages. That is why the housewife suffering from a painful heart ailment rises to it and above it and gives to her neighbors a glimpse of the true glory of God, a light that "shineth in darkness," a light that will never go out even though she may be long since gone from the scene. That is why the athlete, crippled for life, and knowing pain continually, visits children's hospitals, carrying a football, and imparts some laughter and hope to those who cannot understand the meaning of their pain. And that is why a suffering church through the centuries, and even now in war-torn territories of the world, continues to stand as a bulwark amid the wreckage of everything else around it.

Pain is no enemy. It need not breed isolation and loneliness. It may alter mobility, shrink the circumference of total capability, and sometimes bring tears. But to those who see it through the eyes of faith, who catch something of its meaning in God, who know that He is closest in those hours when it is almost unbearable, and His love is there as perhaps at no other time, these give birth to something that man desperately needs, something that lives on, something of light and life that says loneliness of illness need not be forever.

Let illness be more than calamity, hopelessness, loneliness, isolation, and fear! Rather let it be an entrance into a dimension that, like the alabaster box broken to honor the Son of God, gives forth the pervading fragrance of sweet victory in the end. When this attitude prevails, the loneliness of that illness or that pain need not shrink the life or dampen the spirit. Instead, it but enlarges the focus on humanity and opens the conduits of the soul to allow the pouring out of refreshing hope and life to someone else.

When Jesus says, "Friend, I do thee no wrong," that is what He means. And when anyone accepts the attitude implicit in that promise, he will come to know the wonder of it and the glory of it. And loneliness does not live long in that attitude.

TEN

The Loneliness of Bereavement

It's final.

For right now, in this life, at the very present—this is what strikes so painfully that one who has lost someone precious to death. To stand and view what's left, the inanimateness of a bronze casket containing all of what was once laughter and joy and companionship, is the ultimate in pain to many. It is the beginning of mourning, the excruciating hours of "going it alone," of trying to find meaning in life again.

It is this realization that there is no recall of that one gone that brings the shock. This is the finality of earth's experience. In that moment of realization, many feelings pass through the person or persons who remain and must try now to go on again.

Sometimes the remaining spouse will feel pangs of guilt because of having said wrong things to that one while he or she was alive, perhaps because of kindnesses not rendered, when sharp words were allowed to stand. For these, grief is complicated by a sense of guilt. And further, there is no way now to make up for it—there is only the memory of those things, remaining along with the good moments. Sometimes for these it does not "balance out right"—the guilt overwhelms the memory of the good. It is this mourning that becomes complicated; it is this needless self-punishment that has kept many from ever really recovering from the loss.

For others, loneliness moves in with a smothering pall; that companion, that son, that daughter, that one who filled the horizon of the home, of life itself, and made all the struggles worthwhile, is gone forever. For these, loneliness may prevent acceptance of the loss. Some spend endless days picking over familiar objects that belonged to him or her. Some refuse to let any of these go; clothes are allowed to remain where they were; dresser drawers are kept as he or she kept them, with all the trinkets, jewelry, even parking tickets, and receipts with his or her familiar signature on them. These are tearfully viewed every day in some kind of desperate attempt to find the pulse and breath of that one gone.

Again, others wander around the house aimlessly, still looking, still expecting that he or she will appear any moment. Some have awakened at night, sure they heard the familiar voice, and have taken to conversation with the unseen, with empty darkness. Many, even the strongest, never stop crying through the long night hours, for there is the consciousness of emptiness here now; the house no longer harbors the presence, the odors, the familiar contour of the one who dominated the personality of the home and those in it.

The danger in extended mourning that refuses to accept the loss of one gone is that bitterness can set in. Soon there comes the inevitable questioning: Why me? Why him? Why her? These are all human reactions to man's refusal to accept what is the inevitable—separation by death. Even divorced people, those who have been abandoned by a mate, have known this kind of mourning. As one man said, "I maybe could live with this better if she had died—but to know she is not far away, with someone else, to know rejection by her, that I was not adequate to fulfill her life—this to me is almost worse. The times of sorrow and mourning are painful, and one can come close to bitterness in this experience."

Yet who is to say which of these "disconnections" from one loved is more painful? It would seem, however, that those divorced, left behind, manage much more quickly to pick up life again. But for those who have lost one to death, there is the ever-present realization that he is not here, there is never going to be a time to see him again. It is this pain that is probably more acute than the other.

All these reactions to the loss of a loved one are normal. They are a part of the suffering that goes with the life-and-death cycle. Loneliness will be there, sometimes guilt, sometimes months of heaviness and the lack of desire to pick up and go again.

Mourning becomes abnormal when it is allowed to remain, to be coddled forever, so that life is not life for the remaining one, and there is that "strange longing to depart and be where he (or she) is." Some have allowed the shock to strike them so hard that sometimes within months they too succumb to death, their heart and spirit refusing to go on, choosing rather to be gone and hoping to meet the one departed and know again that joy that once was.

A fifty-one-year-old man, three months after losing his wife in a car accident, died of a heart attack. He had never had heart problems and was in perfect health all his life.

One week after the death of her husband, a woman at sixty-three died of a stroke. Two months after the death of her daughter at nineteen of leukemia, the mother at thirty-eight died in her sleep from a blood clot in the lung.

The shock of being forever separated from someone dear and close for some cannot be absorbed. There is simply no "point in going on."

Jean Rosenbaum and Veryl Rosenbaum perhaps summed it up accurately when they commented:

Mourning . . . is more than the purging of grief. It is the psychological burying of the dead. If you do not bury the dead, you have to carry them in your life. How long do you suppose mourning should take? Two years is not an overlong time. . . .

On the other hand, a grief prolonged beyond a reasonable period of mourning may be motivated by self-pity and self-dramatization—an unconscious pleading for continuance of attention and expression of sympathy.[1]

The inevitability of death is not always sure comfort when it occurs to someone close. The "separation anxiety" is acute. It may be true that acceptance of death must come; even all inanimate things erode and crumble. But that is little comfort to the man or woman, the wife or husband, who must face straight into it and try to keep from collapsing under the sheer immensity of it.

Death then is the final insult to man. It is the ultimate in human tragedy. That is because, of course, the individual never anticipates it. In the background of their minds all people know that "death is as sure as taxes." All mankind is fully aware that it has to end some time, that life is not an endless going around many times. But there is still no heart preparation for it. Age comes on, the winter drafts creep in, the signs of what must be that last confrontation with a fading body and life are all too evident. It is a certain grace of God that men and women, knowing this, can maintain some decorum, some sense of dignity in the realization. But when it finally strikes within the intimacy of one's life, there is no "sense of decorum"; at that moment something precious has shattered, and the grave seems to be a mockery to all that has lived.

But again some insist on facing death with grim stoicism. This perhaps is even more pathetic. The face remains locked in the shadows of what has occurred, and there is no break, no sign of mourning. There is only the fight to maintain that dignity that characterized the life of that one now gone. This feeling of having to pose some image of equanimity, of tearlessness even, is a denial of what grief is intended to do.

About this contradiction, the Rosenbaums said, "In America there is an ambivalent attitude toward mourning and toward death itself. In a land where planned obsolescence of all material objects is the rule, there seems to be no room for death. In a land where violence and sudden death are constant factors, there is no time for mourning. It is these contradictions that make death in this country so difficult to accept and to mourn."[2]

Sometimes the Christian, who feels he or she must demonstrate confidence in eternal life, that this death is only temporary, feels he must maintain a "spiritual decorum" lest his faith be judged. Tears then become a contradiction of the hope.

Yet tears are an honest expression of love. Stoicism in the midst of grief is out of synchrony with the cycle of life and death and mourning. Tears show honesty, that the human emotion is there, that it expresses itself, as all of those who stand by expect.

The father who lost his thirteen-year-old son in a drowning accident kept himself calm during the wake and the funeral, dry-eyed, and posing an image of total acceptance of the loss. He kept that pose until he reached the graveside, and then in the mounting realization that this was his last "good-bye," he broke. But rather than show his tears to those mourning with him, he left the graveside quickly, almost as if embarrassed by showing any grief, as if it might cancel his sure conviction that God had done things according to His purpose, even in death. In his refusal to show his grief, he went on to repress it for years, avoiding any conversation about his son, refusing to dwell at any time on his death. Years later, the curse of depression commanded his soul, so much so that he seemed to shrink as a man, until one evening at forty-four years of age he, as his wife said, "turned over in bed and with a long sigh, died."

As the Rosenbaums put it so aptly:

> The mourning process should be fully indulged. Grief is the highest tribute to love. Tears are balm to the crushed spirit. They help heal the wounds of sadness . . . those who put off their grief will pay dearly for their repressed emotions. As long as five, ten and 20 years later these repressed emotions of unspent grief have been known to erupt in the form of massive depression or painful psychosomatic illness known to psychologists as pathological mourning.[3]

There is loss in death that the Christian, as much as those who do not have the hope of eternal life, must face and accept. That companion is gone—at least for now. The loss is there. What lies ready to be lowered into the earth, that one who gave joy and laughter, is gone. At that point, the acceptance of that finality, and the accompanying expression of loss, is the beginning of healing for that torment in grief.

Jesus' weeping over the death of Lazarus is even more amazing in light of the fact that He was going to bring him back from the grave anyway (John 11:35). So why the tears? Because at that point He demonstrated His human identification with those who had lost someone close. To remain quite blasé about it, in light of His power to command the forces of death, would only have communicated a false relationship to those who did weep. The point of pain was felt in His own humanity, and He responded as a man in grief to that situation. Why then does the Christian at times avoid such demonstrations of grief?

Contrarily, Job represented a rather ambivalent attitude toward the sudden death of his entire family. At one point he made his great proclamation of faith in God by saying, "Though He slay me, yet will I trust in Him" (Job 13:15). That was a tremendous statement, truly out of the honesty of his heart. But then he took a peculiar pattern of mourning by sitting on an ash heap and accumulated counselors who put the responsibility for the death of his family on him. Job needed comfort, not condemnation. Sometimes people will seek those who will try to expiate their guilt, if they perhaps feel responsible for someone's death; this is no comfort.

When a person is suffering the shock of grief, what is needed is not a lot of words, something to rationalize death or give a well-intended, but too often cruel, "Well, it was God's will." When a young teenager is killed by a drunken driver, to try to comfort the suffering father by saying, "It is God's will," almost comes as a mockery. True, there is a will of God that works in the mystery of life and death, but in that moment mourning parents need more than that.

In fact, sometimes the less said the better. One man who had lost his eighteen-year-old son in a tobogganing accident remembers sitting in the funeral home, sensing his own acute loss and loneliness. Friends came by and whispered words from Scripture and such things as, "God understands your sorrow." None of that, though well-intended, really assuaged his sense of loss and grief. Then someone came and sat down next to him and put an arm around his shoulder. He said nothing. "But there was comfort in the gesture," the man recalls. "I felt some release in the sense of knowing someone knew what I was feeling and that words would only compound the grief."

People mean well, of course. No one is to be blamed for attempting to give a rationale for death or to inject some word of hope. But there are times when a man (or woman) alone in sorrow needs only a touch, a gesture, or someone to sit quietly beside him and share in the grief.

The word for the mourning one is to let the loneliness come. Let the tears come. It is no denial of the promise of God that there is eternal life, and that the parting is not forever. But in this moment when a man or woman feels the fragility of his own heart that seems ready to break, it is time to use the safety valves God has provided for healing.

In the end, the loneliness of loss must be faced realistically. Time cannot heal the individual who refuses to allow God and time together to affect the bruised inner landscape. The individual has to go on that journey of healing alone. When Jesus said, "Lo, I am with you always," He meant it just as much for those mourning as for those commissioned to some far-off mission field. When the Bible says, "God shall wipe away all tears," it is not referring just to the future millennia, when death is no more. It is as much giving comfort in the fact that He will be the strength and power of the crushed soul in mourning here and now.

Somewhere within the sanctuary of the Christian's soul is that voice of the Spirit that says, "It is not finished. Death has not won. There is yet another day when those who have left you will be united again with you." It is future, to be sure. But many a man and woman in the faith has come out of the deep pit of loneliness in loss by that comfort. For in the midst of tears and loneliness, the Christian as never before can look beyond the "disconnection" from a loved one who has gone and see a comradeship of Christ that holds precious promise. The weak and the frail, the strong and the hearty, can know that mysterious power of healing if they but look for it. It is to know the full meaning of "Yea, though I walk through the valley of the shadow—*thou art there*" (Psalm 23:4, author's paraphrase). Whether one is going through the shadows of death or trying to recover from the loss of someone else, He is there.

It is in this suffering of mourning that the individual comes to learn the great power of finally knowing gladness again. As Karl Barth once put it, "The generation that has no great anguish on its heart will have no great music on its lips."

One woman, who had lost her husband and all four children to a tornado in Michigan, spent months in aimless and futile attempts to try to pick up and live again. Many were kind and comforting. But the pall of mourning remained, clinging to her spirit day after day. Her one prayer daily was, "Lord, give me some reason to rise again and do Your bidding, whatever it may be."

One cold winter morning she awoke early as usual, but aware of a different sound outside. Getting up, she went to the back door and there found a little white puppy, shivering and crying against the cold. For a moment she was startled, wondering to whom it belonged. But then she picked it up and held it close, saying, "Aw, you've lost your mother, and there is nowhere to go."

In that moment of strange communion with the pup, the woman later said, "Suddenly it was as if my husband and the boys had sent me something special, something that needed care, something that would die if I did not care for it. At any other time I would simply have put the dog in a pound. But on this day I sensed 'something of helplessness in that little ball of fur. Maybe it was all too simple, but my own suffering for the moment led me to reach out gently to this forlorn little creature. My heart had been broken, but for that moment a sense of gladness had come in. I was needed again, if for nothing else than to nourish this poor thing to health. Did God send a pup in answer to my prayer? I don't know. All I know is that that little dog became a joy to me, filling my lonely hours—and I realized then that if I could succor an animal in need, I had come a far enough distance to heal others in like suffering. On that day I came to a new awareness that I could go on—remembering those I had lost, yes, but also realizing that I had a life to fill and a service to give."

Yes, "God shall wipe away all tears" and "still leave us glad." On that, the lonely mourning soul can take hope in the reality of life that must go on. And as there is the embracing of God in tears, there comes the morning when all tears cease, and the sun comes in again. Something forever shall remain of the loss of that one so close, but instead of its being a cross too heavy to bear, it now becomes the source of new sensitivity to life, to the suffering of others.

For as Tennyson wrote, "The shell must break before the bird can fly." And further,

> O yet we trust that somehow good
> Will be the final goal.

That is why Paul could shout triumphantly, though his own death was near, "O death, where is thy sting? O grave, where is thy victory?" (1 Corinthians 15:55). For those who remain, the trumpet sound of that sure victory is the same. It is on this that mourning dies on the vine; it is on this that the child of God can rise to a morning in the peace that all is well. In the void there will come new life to fill it; the open wound will heal, and the scar tissue of pain will be covered with the fresh skin of resurgent life.

And to this Tennyson said:

> Behold, we know not anything;
> I can but trust that good shall fall
> At last—far off—at last, to all,
> And every winter change to spring.

Then let it happen, and be glad for what is yet to come, when mourning shall be turned to joy, when life again is lived as it should be lived, not in loneliness forever, but in new hope for the spring. Those who have left us wish it to be so!

ELEVEN

Loneliness and Self-Discovery

In all the crippling effects of loneliness that the individual himself allows to be so, there is still the necessity for aloneness, or what is more accurately called "solitude."

Many people cannot distinguish between loneliness, aloneness, and solitude, confusing them as being detrimental to the human spirit. Loneliness is a "separation anxiety" brought on by the feeling of being disconnected, out of touch; it is a loss of intimacy or belonging. Solitude, however, is an aloneness that is, or can be, creative.

As man cannot go through life without some experience of loneliness in one form or the other, so it is that he must also pursue solitude deliberately to, if nothing else, rearrange the order of his own "inner landscape."

Americans, perhaps more than any other people on earth, avoid solitude with as much frenzy as they do loneliness. It is no wonder there are so many exhausted and sick people in a nation where all resources of material and scientific advances are thought to epitomize modern civilization.

Consider the man who decides to go fishing to "get away from it all." He sits on the bank, one knee jiggling nervously, the other foot digging restlessly into the dirt, his hand on the pole twitching in a peculiar kind of convulsiveness. He is really not "getting away from it all." He had taken with him the busy, crowded, whirlwind life he left behind and is even

176

now unable to make this quiet moment work for him in healing power. One could say, as far as he is concerned, that the
fish have it over on him.

Again, there is the writer who goes to his cabin by the lake
to "get away from deadlines and having to create all the time."
But within two days he is dragging out a portable typewriter
and going at it, complaining, "This silence will drive me
crazy!" He is already a worn-out writer who needs more than
anything else a few days in which he can look at the sky,
water, trees, and birds, and let the machinery inside cool
down a bit. But the inability to understand what creativeness
there is in solitude, that it is somehow linked to the "madness
of silence," is to deny the human spirit its vital recharge for
facing the rigors of everyday life.

Solitude is choosing to be alone. Some who go into solitude,
however, allow themselves to feel the same deadly loneliness
described here already. These fear aloneness in any form;
they have come to conclude the experience is something abnormal. That is why so many will insist on having "some
time alone" by going to a summer camp or retreat. Many
times these are run on hectic schedules. Noisy neighbors prevent sleep, while the days never end, with streams of people
jamming dining halls and children shrieking over the failure
to find ketchup for the hot dog. There is no solitude there,
though some feel it is a means to get away from loneliness.
But being lost in a crowd, battered by the noises of humanity,
the individual fails to find solace for the soul. And many times
he or she does not know why, or perhaps is afraid of being
alone with personal thoughts because these seem to be a
source of terror.

But John Milton in *Paradise Lost* said,

In solitude
What happiness, who can enjoy alone,
Or all enjoying, what contentment find?

Solitude is to let the mind and emotions drain away, free
from the demands of others. It is to commune with self, with
the simplicities and beauty of nature. It is to let the mind
wander, flitting here and there aimlessly, never locked into
any great struggle to make closure. It is a time when the landscape is now filled with nonthreatening vestiges of business
left behind, of problems that plague in the daily routines of
what is called "living" in the great American way. It is a time
when God again walks in the midst of the garden, a time when
the sense of His presence is much more acute. It is a time
when the restless torments of a thousand emotional circuits
are quieted, when there comes that "sweet peace" that man
must have to survive the jungle of his own making.

Solitude is not loneliness then, except to the person who
finds all forms of aloneness threatening. Solitude should not
breed melancholia or depression. Being alone for positive
ends is to catch something of the grandeur of those hidden
parts of life that lie quietly beyond the stormy bastions of industry, waiting to be viewed, tasted, embraced.

A woman who had suffered the ravages of divorce, the
monstrous aftermath of court settlements, and the painful experience of separation forever from one she had lived with for
twenty years could only pull herself from total collapse by
running to a place of solitude, which happened to be a motel
room in Florida. There within those four walls, with no great
scenery to fill her tormented mind, she allowed the toxins in
her soul to drain out.

"God was there," she said of the experience. "In it all, I
found that He was not far outside my tragedy. I read books of

all kinds, and I read the Bible over and over, free of anyone's intrusion, except for room service. Slowly the years of hectic living with a husband who bruised and battered my soul to shreds with his unfaithfulness began to fade from my preoccupation. I began to sleep through whole nights for the first time in years. I found each new day inside those walls a time of renewal, a time when my mind was able again to explore new life, new possibilities for the future. The loneliness I had suffered with an unloving man began to fade, and whatever bitterness I had toward him dissolved. I came out of that little motel room ten days later, a woman who had experienced some definite cure inside, where I had hurt the most—I had found a passage in my hurting life that could only lead to something far better ahead."

But is the practice of solitude encouraged enough or even explained adequately to Christian people who have found themselves incapable of taking even five minutes alone without feeling guilty? Group identification is fine. The fellowship of believers is necessary. But who hasn't seen dragged-out saints "pushed to the wire" by group activities, group demands, group suppers, group Bible studies, group bowling, group visitation, or whatever? Yes, there is joy in being with those of like faith. But when "group fatigue" sets in, when the individual finds himself or herself unable to cultivate the presence of God or know some sense of solitary communion with Him, something is lost.

Jesus Himself told his disciples, "Come . . . apart [get away from it all] . . . and rest awhile" (Mark 6:31). One can be sure that "rest," even for the twelve, was not a drill on Bible memory work or a lecture on evangelistic strategy. One would have to assume that those men "rested" by lying prone on the soil of those quiet Judean hills, each man with his thoughts, while the Lord Himself took the time to refresh His own soul, pushed by the demands of His hour of destiny.

The president of a Bible college in the eastern United States felt that his student body needed to know something of this "creative solitude with God." So he announced that at ten o'clock the following morning, classes scheduled for that time would be cancelled, and each student was to find a quiet place on campus and simply meditate for one hour. There was considerable confusion among many students who did not know exactly how to handle a "free hour" out of the schedule. Some wandered aimlessly, not really knowing what a "quiet place" was, or where to find it.

The president was later shocked to find that more than half of those students, given that hour to be with God and their own thoughts, could not hold out. Many gave up and wended their way to Ping Pong tables and the coffee shop, unable apparently to endure personal solitude on a campus that was so group oriented.

As Walker puts it:

> Our noblest aspirations and our finest hopes are born in solitude. Committee meetings seldom are creative, and the contemporary interest in "brainstorming" in groups is valuable only if members of the group have done their homework in solitude. The insights of our solitude may be sharpened and clarified in groups, but the seeds of thought are sowed in silence.
>
> Only when we are alone are we able to sense the magic of our mysterious universe and capture something of its meaning. In quietness the saints and sages of the past whisper in our listening ears and we hear the "still, small voice" of yesterday and the day before. In the brooding silence of our solitude we digest our own experience and discover the significance of pain and suffering, joy and peace.[1]

Sometimes the church, probably mostly by default, will create an ironic situation in her effort to provide some place that is strictly for solitude. One large church decided to set off a room for private meditation. It was designed for that frenetic saint who, perhaps after an hour of Sunday school teaching, felt the shredding of nerves in the bedlam or for anyone else who might feel the need to get away from the "madding crowd." It is of interest that, two years later, though the room was still marked with a sign that said "The quiet place," now there were mimeograph machines, two cluttered desks where the ushers counted the offering, and four file cabinets to store the church's overflow of correspondence. The "quiet place" had become a non sequitur to the necessary business of the church. The one place then where a torn humanity, even among the saints, might find a place to meditate, in solitude before God, had succumbed to the demands of group enterprise.

How is one to sort out the myriads of messages crossing the brain in a single day unless somehow they become intelligible in the precious moment of solitude? How is the idea of the immensity of God, often expounded in heavy doctrinal preaching or teaching, ever to be absorbed by the finite mind unless there is time alone for Him to come within the limitation of human reasonings.

One prisoner of war in Vietnam related that in the terror of solitary confinement he found that all the Bible passages he had memorized in years past, but which had not seemed to penetrate in application, suddenly became enlarged into life-saving power in the lonely prison cell. Solitude "became my friend, when the enemy thought it would break me. That solitary time opened my mind and heart to dimensions that I had never known in the safety of the group."

Wordsworth as a writer did not remove himself from the concourses of life, but he knew the power of solitude when he wrote:

> I am not one who much or oft delight
> To season my fireside with personal talk . . .
> Better than such discourse doth silence long,
> Long, barren silence square with my desire;
> To sit without emotion, hope, or aim,
> In the loved presence of my cottage-fire
> And listen to the flapping of the flame,
> Or kettle whispering its faint under-song.

Solitude is a kind of aloneness then that brings self-discovery. It allows the mind to untangle itself, the emotions to cool, and with this comes a new awareness of self. It is not to be avoided, but rather pursued. It is not crippling loneliness, except for those who wish or allow it to be that. Rather, even when solitude sometimes brings a sense of loneliness, this in itself is not deadly.

Loneliness—apart from all the crippling it can bring if allowed to enlarge within the heart and mind—is really a healthy means to discovering the need for love. There is a kind of "positive loneliness" within solitude that brings a person to value self and others as never before. The man or woman who seeks solitude, feels some loneliness, and then in terror runs back to the crowd has lost something intended for healing.

As Moustakas said:

> Loneliness has a quality of immediacy and depth, it is a significant experience—one of the few in modern life—in which man communes with himself. And in such communion man comes to grips with his own being. He discovers life, who he is, what he really wants, the meaning of his existence, the

true nature of his relations with others. He sees and realizes for the first time truths which have been obscured for a long time. His distortions suddenly become naked and transparent. He perceives himself and others with a clearer, more valid vision and understanding. In absolutely solitary moments man experiences truth, beauty, nature, reverence, humanity.[2]

Solitude and its accompanying sense of healthy loneliness bring confrontation with self. Sometimes it is painful. But mostly the awareness leads to a new sense of value, a new sense of responsibility toward others. That time to think and pray alone is a time when the Spirit searches quietly and speaks quietly. And from that communion emerges a creativeness that changes the person and changes his entire panorama of relationships.

The president of a large Christian publishing firm was once ordered by his doctor to take a week alone somewhere and "get yourself together." The president was shocked. He had never been alone in his life, and he was proud of it. He always had a company, his own, with 115 people in it; he always had social times, dinner parties, and was considered one of the "who's who" in the community. "Take the time," the doctor insisted, "or face a serious collapse."

The president grudgingly took the order. He went off to his lodge in Maine, where he had always entertained other businessmen during his vacations. Now it was all to himself. For days he paced up and down the front porch, nervously, longing for his briefcase, eager to call back to the office, but unfortunately there was no phone service. He wanted to go to town, call his wife, and ask her to "bring up the gang, and let's have some fellowship." He still does not know why he did not, except, as he said, "I felt that somehow I had to en-

dure this, this being alone, this strange feeling of isolation."
Four days of fidgeting and fuming went by; on the fifth, when
he had decided to drive back home, he was sitting on his front
steps whittling a piece of wood for want of something to do.

"Suddenly I looked up, and a flock of geese lifted off the
lake in front of me and soared upward, gathering into forma-
tion for their journey south. I experienced right then a strange
pang of loneliness, as if I were being left behind, rejected. I
watched them fly on into their formations until they were
gone out of sight—and then I suddenly felt remorse. I thought
of the many people in my thirty-five years in the company
whom I had let go, people whom I had cut off for one pica-
yune reason or another. Suddenly I saw their faces, faces that
pleaded to remain, to stay with the group, to be a part of the
work. I felt my own loneliness then and realized for the
first time what theirs must have been like to be rejected.

"I sat on that porch and cried, that stick of wood in my
hand a counterpart of my feeling of bankrupt self. Something
happened on that fifth day; I faced myself and what I had
done in thirty-five years of handling people in a Christian
company. I had come to know loneliness for the first time,
and now it brought me to a whole new sense of love for every
child of God. I had never had a prayer session like that in my
life; it lasted for hours, between my tears of repentance.

"When it was over, I got into my car and drove home. I
was never the same again in my relationship with people. I
had caught God's dimension of the smallest of them as precious, not only to Him but to me. Loneliness in solitude
taught me something gigantic about myself and others. I
learned in that experience simply to love."

Solitude, then, even with the accompanying pangs of loneliness, can be creative. The self-discovery that can be found

only when alone is imperative for mental, emotional, and spiritual health. God speaks much more to the person who has sought solitude for spiritual refreshment and renewal than He does to one in a busy crowd where there is often preoccupation with matters peripheral to inner growth.

For all the costly experiences resulting from loneliness already covered in this book, there is one predominant fact that must emerge: God is never far outside those experiences. In the final analysis, He is the all-in-all, and because of that no child of God should ever allow aloneness or loneliness to dictate the course of life or experience.

For the one who holds God close and knows what that "still small voice" means in the dark hours, there is that promise, "Lo, I am *with you always*, even to the end of the age" (Matthew 28:20, NASB, author's emphasis).

When Robert L. became blind at twenty-two as a result of insulin shock, his whole landscape was completely wiped out. He was plunged into a world of darkness, pushed into a corner of his "inscape," forced now to face into what could be a life of crushing loneliness. For months he fought his way through to a new, different, and almost totally helpless way of life. But his mother stated that in all that time she never sensed any moments of depression, nor did he complain.

As Robert put it, "The first weeks were the strangest—almost terrifying. It was like being put into a box and having the lid nailed down over me. And yet as time went on, I began to realize I was not alone in my darkness. As I turned inward, because there was really nowhere else to go, there was God, walking in the middle of that darkness. He was even more clear then than when I had all my senses. I had read of people who had gone blind and how they withdrew to their inner world that offered no solace. I found, however, that my inner world suddenly became alive with His presence. He had always been there, throughout my life, but only now did I see Him standing within the shadows. Every day became one filled with expectation from Him, and He never failed to show up. Without Him there, I am sure I would have wound up in serious depression."

What Robert L. experienced in the loneliness of his world, the realization that God was in the midst of it, is a lesson to those who, even with all their senses, need to learn.

It need not take blindness to prove His presence, or any other catastrophic experience. Whenever the individual feels alone or loneliness, the landscape seems to blur; but at that moment the "inscape" becomes the seedbed of life and companionship in God. In those times of solitude and the loneliness that comes with it, He is ready to reveal Himself. It is but for the individual to watch and wait for Him with expectancy; He comes, in His time; He always comes.

Loneliness need not be a crippler then. It need not lead to despair. Loneliness is bound to come to everyone's life sooner or later through the earthshaking experiences all mankind is heir to. The secret is in understanding that it is not a process for ill but is an opportunity for God to show Himself as He perhaps cannot do when the landscape becomes too crowded.

It is this vein, converting loneliness into an opportunity for Him within the "inscape," that Clark Moustakas referred to when he said: "Being lonely and being related are dimensions of an organic whole, both necessary to the growth of the individuality and to the deepening value and enrichment of friendship Let there be loneliness, for where there is loneliness, there is also love, and where there is suffering, there also is joy.'"

The remainder must be repeated often in the experience of

loneliness, as the Lord gave it Himself: "He shall give you another Comforter, that he may abide with you for ever" (John 14:16). If the individual had no one else on earth with whom to fellowship, that "Comforter" within would be enough. And it is because He works within to reveal Himself to those who are lonely that one can confidently say with Anna Monroe, "Loneliness is only an opportunity to cut adrift and find yourself." And with that, certainly to find Him.

The truth so many have proved in their lives must be nailed down: for that one who walks the solitary road, God remains the same in the promise of His presence. For those who have suffered broken relationships, rejection or loss, or whatever else contributes to loneliness, He is always there. He can be found in the empty places as well as in those crowded land-scapes. He can be found in the quiet forests of solitude or in the faces of those who pass by in the busy concourse of life, those who gladly accept the embrace of someone who cries for intimacy. He may be found in the solitary place where only nature traces His footsteps and where there is a communion mystifying but beautiful. Yes, he may be found in the lin of industry, in the roar of human traffic, which has its own peculiar chemistry for isolating individuals.

Look for Him then! He alone is the balm for healing, whether for physical pain or for the perplexing pain of an empty "inscape." Even if that landscape becomes barren, He is never far away. And if the struggle seems long, it is not that He is not there. It is faith alone that cries out, "He will come! Do not despair; He will come! He is there even now, but the dull vision, the preoccupation with aloneness and the pain of it keeps Him hidden. Let the eyes of faith behold Him, and then let the 'inscape' be filled with His presence and glory!"

Robert Browning, who knew something of this struggle with God, phrased it best when he said:

> I go to prove my soul!
> I see my way as birds their trackless way.
> I shall arrive! What time, what circuit
>   first,
> I ask not: but unless God send his hail
> Or blinding fireballs, sleet or stifling snow,
> In some time, his good time, I shall arrive:
> He guides me and the bird. In his good
>   time.

Then so be it!

Notes

CHAPTER 1

1. James J. Lynch in an interview with Christopher Anderson, *People*, 22 August 1977, p. 30.
2. Ibid.
3. William Sadler, Jr., "Loneliness," *Science Digest* 78, no. 1 (July 1975): 60-61.
4. Harold Blake Walker, *To Conquer Loneliness* (New York: Harper & & Row, 1966), p. 2.
5. Ibid., p. 4.
6. Ibid.
7. Ira J. Tanner, *Loneliness: The Fear of Love* (New York: Harper & Row, 1973), p. 16.
8. Paul Tournier, *Escape from Loneliness* (Philadelphia: Westminster 1976), p. 23.

CHAPTER 2

1. Robert S. Weiss, "Loneliness—The Experience of Emotional and Social Isolation" (Cambridge, Mass.: Massachusetts Institute of Technology, 1973), p. 76.
2. Ibid., pp. 80-81.
3. Ibid., p. 66.
4. William Sadler, Jr., "Loneliness," *Science Digest* 78, no. 1 (July 1975): 60-61.
5. Harold Blake Walker, *To Conquer Loneliness* (New York: Harper & Row, 1966), p. 20.
6. Ibid., p. 31.
7. Ibid., p. 30.
8. Ibid., p. 29.
9. Sadler, p. 65.
10. Ibid.
11. Walker, p. 33.
12. Jeremy Seabrook, *Loneliness* (New York: Universe, 1975), pp. 7-8.

CHAPTER 3

1. Jean Rosenbaum and Veryl Rosenbaum, *Conquering Loneliness* (New York: Hawthorne, 1973), pp. 125-26.
2. Sören Kierkegaard, as quoted by Clark E. Moustakas, in *Portraits of Loneliness and Love* (Englewood Cliffs, N.J.: Prentice-Hall, 1974), p. 11.
3. Moustakas, p. 28.
4. Martin Buber, as quoted by Moustakas, p. 69.

CHAPTER 4

1. Thomas Wolfe, as quoted by Clark E. Moustakas in *Portraits of Loneliness and Love* (Englewood Cliffs, N.J.: Prentice-Hall, 1974), p. 45.
2. Harold Blake Walker, *To Conquer Loneliness* (New York: Harper & Row, 1966), p. 160.
3. Moustakas, p. 41.

CHAPTER 5

1. Clark E. Moustakas, *Portraits of Loneliness and Love* (Englewood Cliffs, N.J.: Prentice-Hall, 1974), p. 15.
2. Thomas Dooley, as quoted by Agnes W. Dooley in *Promises to Keep* (New York: Farrar, Straus & Giroux, 1962), pp. 271-72.
3. Harold Blake Walker, *To Conquer Loneliness* (New York: Harper & Row, 1966), p. 81.
4. Jim Elliot, as quoted by Elisabeth Elliot in *Shadow of the Almighty* (New York: Harper, 1958), p. 152.
5. Ibid., p. 249.

CHAPTER 6

1. Jean Rosenbaum, and Veryl Rosenbaum, *Conquering Loneliness* (New York: Hawthorne, 1973), p. 18.
2. Harold Blake Walker, *To Conquer Loneliness* (New York: Harper & Row, 1966), p. 2.
3. Ibid., p. 106.
4. David Reisman, *The Lonely Crowd: A Study of the Changing American Character* (New Haven, Conn.: Yale U. Press, 1950), p. 130.
5. Ibid., p. 130.
6. Walker, p. 107.

CHAPTER 7

1. Paul Tournier, *Escape from Loneliness* (Philadelphia: Westminster, 1976), p. 22.
2. Suzanne Gordon, *Lonely in America* (New York: Simon & Schuster, 1976), p. 110.
3. Ibid.
4. Ibid. p. 111.
5. Tournier, p. 42.
6. Ibid., p. 43.
7. S. I. Hayakawa, as quoted by Clark E. Moustakas in *Portraits of Loneliness and Love* (Englewood Cliffs, N.J.: Prentice-Hall, 1974), p. 27.
8. Moustakas, p. 86.
9. Tournier, p. 165.
10. Seneca *Epistles* 4.5.